The Cry  t

My Bali Diary

by
Totty Ellwood

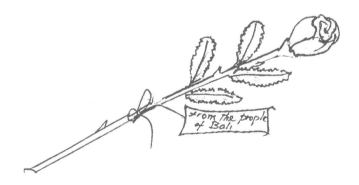

from the people of Bali

*No bomb that ever burst
Shatters the crystal spirit*

George Orwell

Published 2003 by Peridot Press,
a division of John Catt Educational Ltd
Great Glemham, Saxmundham, Suffolk IP17 2DH
Tel: +44 (0) 1728 663668 Fax: +44 (0) 1728 663415
E–mail: info@peridot.co.uk Internet: http://www.peridot.co.uk

Opinions expressed in this publication are those of the contributors, and
are not necessarily those of the publishers or the sponsors. We cannot
accept responsibility for any errors or omissions.

The Sex Discrimination Act 1975. The publishers have taken all reason-
able steps to avoid a contravention of Section 38 of the Sex
Discrimination Act 1975. However, it should be noted that (save where
there is an express provision to the contrary) where words have been
used which denote the masculine gender only, they shall, pursuant and
subject to the said Act, for the purpose of this publication, be deemed to
include the feminine gender and vice versa.

A CIP catalogue record for this book is available from the British
Library.

ISBN: 0901577 97 9

Designed and typeset by Peridot Press, a division of John Catt
Educational Limited,
Great Glemham, Saxmundham, Suffolk IP17 2DH

Printed and bound in Great Britain by Bell and Bain Ltd, Glasgow,
Scotland.

Contents

Acknowledgements

First and foremost thank you to Jonathan Evans and Derek Bingham at John Catt for publishing the diary. Thank you to my editors, Mother and Tobias. Thank you to all the people who supported me in Bali, Aldbury, Vietnam and in Penang. I am particularly grateful to Fiona, Stephanie and Petra for their support via e-mail communication as well as friends in Penang like Leighton and Rachel; all helped me towards the path of actually putting pen to paper.

There were so many friends and families going through their own tragedy in Bali at that time; this story is a record of events from my point of view and does not reflect the feelings or views of others.

A great many people have supported each member of our family in different ways, helping us individually and collectively get through the initial pain. We are truly grateful and I hope that in reading this diary they will realise how important every message, act or gesture was.

I initially wrote the diary because it helped me express my feelings as each dreadful day proceeded. I then decided that I wanted Felicity and Freddy to know what happened to their uncle, Jonathan.

My family have been my rock, my anchor. Thank you to my husband, Matthew who took care of me and put up with my mood swings. Thank you also to Felicity and Freddy who just by being there, two innocent little beings, made me look forward instead of backwards.

Totty Ellwood

The Crystal Spirit

Prologue – Summer 2002

If you look at the world from far, far away it is all connected. Lands connected by oceans, by the air that we breathe, polluted or clean, by dark overcast weather, by tropical brightness. Now narrow your view and look in closer you will see more connections, mountains, valleys, cities, villages, all varying in size. Take an even closer look you can see millions of people going about their daily business, good people, bad people, lonely people, the happy, the rich, the poor, busy people and bored people. Like ants building an anthill they are connected as they move – mixing, parting, interacting, fighting, loving, procreating, eating, drinking, just being.

Somewhere, someone is standing in a travel agents glancing through a brochure. Their eye catches a beautiful sunset in Bali. Elsewhere a man is organising a rugby sevens tournament; a woman is planning a secret surprise trip for her partner; two girls are counting their savings towards the holiday of a life-time. Somewhere, someone is packing for a business conference, someone else is booking their flight.

Somewhere, someone is making a bomb.

It is a bomb that will blast into the lives of thousands of innocent people in an attempt to change the world. But the bomb will not change the world, it will ruin it for some, it will cause upheaval for others but, for most in the world, it will pass by as another piece of tragic news that makes the headlines. For the world is so big and, despite being connected, people will still go about their daily business.

We will still get up each day, go to work, eat, drink, argue, love and care. The world will still turn. But for some the world will never be the same.

Somewhere someone is planning a trip to Bali and somebody else is making a bomb.

Introduction

The phone rang at three in the morning. I knew it meant trouble. Sara Beck the BBC's Asia Bureau Chief was on the line. "There's been a bomb explosion in Bali, not sure how many are dead but it looks bad." "Bomb explosion in Bali?"I wiped the sleep from my eyes. She said the next flight isn't until 9.30, I could get a few more hours kip. Needless to say I didn't. Too much was going on inside my head. I just lay in bed thinking who on earth would want to attack Bali? I'd spent the New Year there seeing in 2002.That balmy December 31st night was magical. I was with my wife Catherine, a bar full of happy revellers, and plenty of champagne. At the time I remember thinking I must be one of the luckiest foreign correspondents alive to have somewhere so extraordinarily beautiful right in the middle of my patch.

Who would want to attack Bali? Maybe it was just an awful gas explosion or something. Sure bombs do go off in other parts of Indonesia, planted by any number of suspects. Disgruntled nationalists angry at the loss of East Timor. Army officers-supporters of the one-time dictator Suharto-angry at their loss of power and prestige. Opponents of the President Megawati Sukarno Putri trying to make a point. Guerillas fighting for independence for any number of provinces. Yes in Jakarta, Aceh, but Bali? It's a little island full of Hindus and Australian backpackers!

I touched down in the capital Denpasar with Sara and cameraman Jone Cheng having made that 9.30 flight. I'm the BBC's Asia Correspondent with responsibility for getting stories on the domestic UK TV bulletins from the region. Sara went off to try and find a base for our operations for the next week, while Jone and I hung around the airport waiting to talk to any holidaymakers who were leaving because of what happened. Sure enough we found a British couple with their young son. They'd arrived two days earlier, were due to stay for a week, but were leaving on the next plane. They told me they couldn't take the risk that another bomb might go off. I still couldn't believe they were talking about Bali.

Our next task was to get to the bomb site, the Kuta area of the island, a favourite haunt for Australian tourists. What I saw left me speechless. Acres of twisted metal and fallen masonry had been cordoned off by the police. I'd covered the war in Afghanistan the year before and this looked worse than Kabul! It was clear by now that it was a bomb attack, two in fact had gone off and scores of people had been killed. The Sari

Nightclub and Paddy's Bar were popular with tourists. Foreigners were the target of the killers. I recorded a piece to camera making these points and then headed for the hospital.

I'd just seen what the explosions had done to a bar and nightclub. Now I saw what they did to flesh and bone. The wards were crowded with people, some horribly burned, caught in the fireball. In room 205 we found one man with appalling injuries, but who managed to tell us what he saw. Everything we filmed that day made it onto the evening news.

In all we were in Bali for just over a week, reporting on the investigation into who had planted the bombs, talking to the relatives and friends of those who were killed…foreigner and local. It was in the middle of all this that I met Tobias Ellwood. I'm looking for a story and he has one to tell. It also transpires that we have mutual friends back in Battersea. We hit it off.

Tobias had flown to Bali to claim the body of his brother Jon. He'd been positively identified, so you'd think Tobias could take him home? Wrong! It was his fight and that of his sister Totty to get Jon's body back to the UK, that formed the basis of some of the reports we filmed.

I tried to capture it, but could only scratch the surface of the grief Tobias, Totty and so many others were feeling. Not just because they'd lost relatives and friends, but because that anguish was compounded by red tape. The diary you're about to read far more eloquently than a two minute news report, brings home their love for their brother and the grief that he's gone.

The last time I was in Bali was at the beginning of August. I was covering the sentencing of the first of the men tried and found guilty for the bombing, for killing Tobias and Totty's brother. Amrozi Bin Nurhasyim is a village car mechanic from East Java. A Moslem extremist who'd bought the van and the explosives used in the attack. He wanted to kill foreigners, people he considered infidels,non-believers. People like Jon Ellwood whom he'd never met, didn't know, but hated anyway. When the court sentenced him to death by firing squad, he turned to the packed public gallery and smiled. He was to become a martyr to his God, to his cause. He was celebrating the deaths of more than two hundred people, and soon his own.

Clive Myrie,
Singapore,
August 2003.

Going to Bali

19 September, 2002

Dear Sheila,

Nice to hear from you!

It's ages since I last heard from you. The summer went by too fast. And with my work at the Pendley Shakespeare Festival I did not see many people in the village this year.

Because of the festival, I arrived back here in Vietnam later than I should have done. Think I got away with it. Am renegotiating my contract for a possible third year of teaching. This will mean a little more money. Otherwise I will be off to another school.

In a couple of weeks I am off to Bali, for a week. A few days holiday before a conference there. This means the school pays for my flights – which is pretty good.

Vietnam has got a little better since I returned. I have started playing a lot more tennis, and am taking lessons. My game has improved no end. Not that I am up to Wimbledon standard! Am going to start aerobics on Monday, so that should be fun. At least I will get to see some women in tights. Knowing my luck, they will all be overweight parents.

This weekend I am off to the seaside with the lower sixth form, for a weekend of work and games. It will be tiring but fun. The school rules state staff are not allowed to drink. So we are all coming up with ingenious ways to smuggle in and consume alcohol. The whole thing is daft and reminds me of being at school myself.

Totty is doing fine in Penang. Mum has just visited her. She was there for about three weeks. Totty has settled in well, although it was a bit of a culture shock when she first arrived. She misses Aldbury – but she will get used to it. I also miss Aldbury, but have got used to being away and always look forward to getting back. Christmas will however be different this year. For the first time ever I am not going to be in Aldbury or with the family. And I won't be in The Trooper on New Year's Eve.

I'm going to Australia for three weeks, to Sydney and then to Melbourne to watch Test cricket on Boxing Day. After that I am off to the Gold Coast to meet friends and have New Year's on the Beach. Having never been I am very excited and looking forward to it.

Hope all is well. Keep practising those dominoes. Will be back next summer for a few matches.

Jonathan.

12th October

The plane journey down to Bali stopped off at Singapore. Unfortunately it was not business class this time. That was saved for long-haul and definitely worth it, in Jonathan's opinion.

He once said to me "I hate flying, so I get very, very drunk on red wine." So on the first leg of his journey, from Vietnam to Bali, he drank copious amounts of wine with his friend and colleague Derek. He purchased a copy of *FHM*, a book and some duty free at the stop over in Singapore and the red wine duly took affect, allowing Jonathan to sleep peacefully on the final two hour flight to Bali.

Landing in Bali is like arriving in most places in Asia: waves of heat envelop you as you descend from the plane, but Jonathan was an Asian veteran by now and used to it.

Jonathan, known to his friends as Jon, was planning to have a good time. He was in Bali for a senior teaching conference for International Schools in East Asia and was representing the International School of Ho Chi Minh City. He had arranged with some former colleagues to arrive a few days early to enjoy the beautiful island and so Mel and Shane Walsh-Till all arrived in Bali armed with tennis racquets, swimming gear and trashy novels which would see them through to the conference in four days time.

Jon was met at the airport by a friendly driver who insisted on calling him 'Mr Jon'. In his Balinese costume, which included a turquoise headscarf and what seemed like a combination of trousers and a dress, the driver negotiated the bustling streets of the capital to the The Melasti Beach Bungalows Hotel, in the tourist area, not far from the airport.

Jon strolled into the hotel in his usual confident manner, signed his hotel chitty and collected his room key, which included a large wooden label marked 227. He followed the guide down to the restaurant where Shane, his wife Mel, and her sister Elissa, were sitting in the restaurant. Mel gave him a big hug. It had been half a year since Jon had seen the couple during a visit to Hong Kong where Shane and Mel worked at the Chinese International School (CIS). Of course Shane and Jon gave each other a manly handshake, accompanied by pleased grins.

The banter of familiar friends ensued – the flight, the hotel: "I've seen better" says Jon. The Hotel was fairly basic with a small restaurant next to the pool. "It's nothing like the Le St Geran Hotel" (where they had once all stayed) Jon observed. They discussed changing hotels.

Jon was not hungry so he shared some of their pizza and ordered a beer while they finished off. All were quite tired, but the joy of the reunion and prospect of a few days holiday before the conference set a very relaxed atmosphere and the conversation eventually turned to the plans for the night.

Jon was a fairly big chap, nearly six foot tall and rather robust. He was developing a beer belly which was a useful place to settle his glass. His usual position, when he was relaxed, was to lean back into his chair, his arms behind his head and his legs crossed, and so he was, chatting away and waiting for his Bin-Tang Beer.

It was now 10pm. The two girls were happy to call it a night. Shane and Jon however, were keen to head into town. Jon dumped his bag in his room and sat on his balcony, looking out into the night sky.

It was a clear night with a panorama of stars twinkling down on the little island of Bali, where, in numerous hotels and cabins, people were getting ready to descend on the bars and clubs. Shane took a few minutes to get ready. Jon did not mind waiting; he was enjoying the ambience of one of the holiday capitals of Asia. Mel shouted across from her balcony: "Jonny, I recorded those CDs for you on mini-disc. I'll give it to you in the morning. See ya in the morning, mate".

She disappeared into her room where Shane could be seen giving her a kiss as he said "I'm not going to be long old mate, we'll just have a few beers and come home."

"That's OK babe, go and catch up with Jonny and I'll see you in the morning. Have a good time. I love you."

And off Jon and Shane went into the night.

They headed straight for the Sari Club, a ten minute walk. Who knows what they talked about: their common past as teachers at the Bavarian International School; catching up on people they knew; where they were; what they were doing. Grand plans for the future; children for Shane;

girlfriends for Jon. Jon was certainly coming of age; happy at work, happy with his social life. But at 37 it was now time to find someone to share it all with.

Passing Paddy's Bar, another popular watering point on their right, they headed for the famous Sari Club opposite. It was the biggest in Bali, a natural attraction to any westerner passing through Bali. There, music blasting out, they would continue to put the world to rights. Leaning against the bar, Jon placed his wallet on the table, getting ready to pay for the round.

The club was packed with tourists, surfers in beach-ware, rugby players recovering from their tournament, honeymooners, travellers, professionals, people from all walks of life. Jelan Legian, the main street of Kuta, was the place to be – good music and a good reputation for dancing, drinking and the essential warm, enticing night atmosphere. Suddenly, just after 11 o'clock, came the first, horrific blast.

From just inside Paddy's Bar there was an ear-splitting explosion. Inside the Sari Club people screamed. Many ran out into the street to see what was going on. They ran straight into the next shower of terror: the killing bomb that slaughtered 204 people, wounded so many more and pointlessly destroyed countless people's lives for ever.

Count aloud to five, count to ten, maybe even count to 30. It can seem an eternity when counting in real time. For our two friends it was 30 seconds of darkness and disorientation followed by confused deafness and asphyxiation. For Jon it ended with something going through his chest and so ultimately to death. Count to 40 and in those short moments Jon's, Shane's and all the unfortunate others' time in this world was over.

****

Ignorance

I am a languages teacher at the International School of Penang, Malaysia. My husband, Matt, and I are house-parents at the school boarding house. We live on the school premises and help look after the children who board. We are having our living-room painted. A Mediterranean, terracotta feel is what I am looking for, even though now we were living in the tropics. Only yesterday I negotiated the price and now the local workers from our school are earning some extra money, saving up for their Deepavali festival celebrations. Matt is rather surprised to discover that we have to move the entire contents of our living-room into the middle, but he agrees. This is my call.

So we spend the afternoon with our two children Freddy (two) and Felicity (three) in the bedroom with our TV and DVD player borrowed from the German department watching, for the tenth time, the cartoon film *Tarzan*. For Matt and me however, the novelty of seeing Tarzan woo Jane has worn off and we lie on the bed and chat, funnily enough about the future. The conversation eventually turns from a discussion to an argument. Time to get out. Fortunately, Tarzan had just finished saving Jane for the tenth time. "Come on Kids, let's go to Gurney". Gurney is a huge air conditioned shopping Plaza, next door to the school, where we pop in to cool off and have an ice-cream. With any luck we will be able to see some painting progress by the time we get back.

At 5.30 pm, we return to see the three workers doing the last layer of rich orange paint. We walk into the vast living-room "Oh my goodness" I exclaim "Oh my God..." says Matt "Wow..." squeaks an excited Felicity "it's orange". It is truly a deep, deep orange.

The phone rings "Oh hi Mum, we've just painted our living-room orange" I burst out before she could say anything. Mum, who lives in Aldbury, Hertfordshire, had visited us and could indeed envisage it straight away, but she wasn't interested.

"Totty, have you seen the news?"

"No."

"There's been a bomb in Bali. You don't think Jonathan is anywhere near it, do you?"

"No, of course not. Anyway he's not due to go until Wednesday, the conference isn't for another week."

"No, I'm sure he was going this Saturday. He rang on Thursday to tell me and I checked his last e-mail. He's left for the conference early."

I had had calls like this before, about other members of my family. My father worked for the UN and Tobias, the younger of my two brothers, was in the army and served in Northern Ireland and Bosnia.

"I didn't even know there was a bomb" (we have had no TV for four months).

"Yes, last night at midnight."

"Don't worry Mum, I'm sure he wasn't there." And I am sure.

Just another bomb, we both think. It happens somewhere in the world and it is not going to affect us. It is something you see on television. It happens to other people.

The boarding house dinner bell rings: "Got to go Mum, dinner's ready, talk to you later"and I hang up.

After dinner, the painters have gone, and our living-room is back to its normal state, except it's orange. "Hey – it's orange. How exciting, it smells all clean. I love it." I exclaim. The 'phone rings.

This time Matt answers; he turns to me. "Totty, it's for you. It's your Mum, something's happened." My heart pounds as I grab the 'phone.

"Totty, Jonathan's missing. I've called the Foreign Office and they now know for sure that he is one of the missing."

"Oh Mum."

"I don't know anything else. I'll call as soon as I do."

I don't know which way to turn, what to do, who to ring or where to go. We have no television. I don't know the scale of the bomb. I know nothing. I rush next door to Jo and Avis, our fellow house parents at the boarding house.

"I'm sorry to bother you, it's my brother, Jonathan, he's been in the bomb."

They know nothing of the bomb either, proving what ignorant lives we can live when we don't see or hear the news. The world could come to an end and you wouldn't even know it. Jon's world had finished and I am unaware.

We watch the news over and over again. BBC World, then over to CNN, then back again. Over and over again BBC World show the inferno of the Sari Club burning in the night. Then it jumps to pictures of bodies being carried out from the wreckage. Bodies lie in rows in white sacks along the side of the road. Then more bodies are taken into ambulances. Is one of them Jon? Maybe he is in a hospital with burns. It shows the Australians flying in and evacuating many wounded. Maybe one of them is Jon? Then they show bodies being carried into trucks. Maybe he is one of them? I try to imagine Jon and absurdly can't understand why I don't know if he is one of them.

The immensity of it all fails to settle. I am sitting right in front of the television screen, it's almost as if I'm trying to see him in the footage. Avis is kindly trying to 'phone the British Embassy in Jakarta. We have no information, maybe he's just missing, in a bar somewhere else. But even my confused senses can work out that this bomb went off 20 hours ago. If he is alive they would have found him by now, he would have told someone his name.

Jo gets an emergency number off the web, but that doesn't work either, nobody answers. The embassy in Jakarta eventually gives us an emergency number. This turns out to be the totally unhelpful Foreign Office number in the UK. What on earth are we doing calling Jakarta for information about the country they are in and being referred back to the UK? No, it seems they have nothing further to report, Jon Ellwood is still missing. I need to do something... I must call my father.

My parents are separated and Dad still lives in Vienna, Austria. I go back next door to call him and his partner answers.

"Is it important?" she asks "He's got gastric flu"

"Just get him, NOW."

A sickly, coughing voice eventually answers.

"Dad, Jon was in the bomb in Bali." Unlike my ignorant self my father knows about the bomb. There isn't anything else to say except to report back as soon as I know anything further.

Dad also 'phones the Foreign Office and the Jakarta Embassy. No-one is answering.

I go back to the television at our neighbours. I return to my kneeling, rocking posture on the floor; watching and waiting for more news. It dawns on me that the best thing will be to go there. After all, of all my family, I am the closest.

I have this pounding inside me; this horrible feeling that won't go away. My insides are whispering to me, "he's dead" but it is all an incomprehensible fog and my brain won't work.

Jo looks up the times of flights. There is one in the morning. Yet I am still waiting for the 'phone to ring and someone, to say "It's alright, he's been found."

The 'phone does ring. It is not the Foreign Office, but Mum. She has spoken to Mel, who has called from Bali, and is looking for both Shane and Jon. She and her sister have been scouring the hospitals. All we can do is wait.

But I can't wait any longer, so I call Mel. The way she answers you can tell she is hoping the same as I am. That it would be the call to say that her husband, Shane is OK.

"Mel, what's happening?"

"We've been to all the hospitals and we can't find him." It is hard to tell whether she's talking about Jon or Shane. It makes no difference though; they are having no success, just horror. She sounds exhausted.

"I'll call as soon as I know – stay strong." I think she is telling herself those two last words.

"You too" I say. Tears are flowing down my cheeks, I am stepping out of the unknown fog into a clarity that spells out the words inside me: Jon was in that bomb and is probably, if not certainly, dead.

I go to bed, going through the motions, cleaning my teeth, putting on my nighty and checking on the children. Matt is already in bed, trying to sleep. I can't sleep. My eyes are wide open, staring at the fan on the ceiling, watching the blades go round and round, moving warm air from one part of the room to another. I hear the occasional motorbike go past in the street. I am thinking of Jon. Thinking of the pictures of the inferno, the bomb, and the bodies. Matt can't sleep either, so I snuggle up to him, as we both fear the worst and cry. Those two words keep rattling around my mind, forbidding sleep as repeatedly they whisper: "he's dead, Jonathan's dead…"

Eventually I find some sleep in the small hours of the morning, although it is little solace as I end up dreaming. My dream is vivid: I have arrived in Bali to look for Jon and I'm on the bus from the airport coming into the main town. It is a desolate almost deserted town. The houses are few and far apart. Everything is dusty and dirty. The sides of the roads are strewn with bodies. My bus is packed full of people, smelly people, fat people, thin people, families, unknown individuals, all on their way to the town centre with their big bags, rocking about in the shoddy bus.

I look out of the window as the outskirts of the town whisk past. I want to get out and look but we are not at the stop yet. I have a sense of foreboding but suddenly out of the corner of my eye I see somebody on the side of the road. "Stop!" I scream at the bus driver. "It's Jon!" I clamber over luggage and people and push my way through the crowded bus. The front door is open and I jump off on to the corner pavement where the big lump of a Jonathan is lying under a cotton sheet. He can't speak but I hold his hand and say "It's OK, I'm here now."

At 7am there is still no call from anyone. Felicity and Freddy get up as usual and Matt tends to their needs as I call Mel. She answers straight away but again she has nothing to report.

"I think I had better come down there" I suggest.

"That would be good" she replies.

I can't avoid the question any longer, I take a deep breath and ask "Mel, do you think they are dead?"

She pauses and then sobs "I think so, Totty, we're going to the morgue this morning".

In some ways Mel only confirms my inner voice for me. Jon's life had ended 32 hours before. Even though I didn't know it then, I was convinced he was dead.

I 'phone Mum to say I'm going to Bali.

"Do you want Tobias to come out?"

"No, I'll be OK".

"Are you sure Totty? He can get a flight tonight".

"Let's see what happens when I get there."

She still doesn't believe the worst has happened.

I 'phone Dad in Vienna. He is also still praying in hope.

"Maybe he's on one of the planes to Australia – we mustn't give up."

But they haven't been speaking to Mel. I know he is dead.

My Head Teacher comes round to offer a lift to the airport but Avis is already getting her car out. I pack my blue rucksack. It is Jon's old rucksack – before he moved to a superior brand. As with many of my things, they are my brother's cast offs. I travel light. A book, which is never opened, $500 in my back pocket, a change of clothes, my swimsuit and my passport.

It is 8 am and just before I leave, I sit Felicity, who is not quite four-years-old, down on the sofa next to me.

"Mummy's got to go away for a while."

"Why?" This is her standard answer for anything incomprehensible.

17

"I've got to go and look after Jonathan."

"Is he sick?"

"Yes and I need to go and take care of him."

My eyes are overflowing.

"Give me a hug, I love you." As I hold her tight and cry, she starts to take in my emotion and looks worried. She digs her head into me. "Love you" she whispers.

****

Mel's Thoughts

Jonny & Tilly (Shane) would have gone to the Sari Club for old times' sake. Tilly went there ten years ago with his best mate. They spent many nights at the Sari Club.

Jonny and Tilly were happy and relaxed, both smiling and laughing in each other's company.

They would have been having a good old chat and there would have been darkness. They would have felt no pain.

Out there in the darkness, out there in the night, two stars shine brighter than a thousand suns. Those stars are Shane and Jon.

****

14th October

At the airport I desperately try to get a ticket. The man at the Singapore Airlines desk attempts to be helpful. "If you go through a travel agent it is much cheaper." He doesn't understand the situation, so I go along to the Malaysia desk.

"My brother was in the bomb, I must get to Bali as soon as possible" This man is more understanding and sorts out a ticket quickly.

I have entered into a world of numbness and act on automatic. Matt and I sit in the airport for two hours waiting for the plane, but really waiting for the worst. As Matt gets me a drink, I pick up a newspaper – *The Star*. Sprawled over three pages are the details of the bomb, graphic pictures of charred bodies, the furnace of fire and details of the bomb's impact on the area. I can't read it. They are only words, but they seem too harsh to take in. It's like looking at an awful wound on someone: you just want to look away. I fold the paper up again, but images of the fire from the television spring back into my mind's eye and I can't eat the breakfast in front of me. Matt doesn't know what to say. I simply sit there shaking and don't communicate. I just want to keep moving, get there, to whatever it is that is waiting for me.

My journey takes me via Kuala Lumpur International Airport. At an internet café I send an e-mail to Mum, Dad and Tobias; "I will find him" I say, my inability to express anything else underlining the powerlessness of it all. I then sit motionless in the waiting area.

The flight to Bali seems to take an eternity. Huddled by the window I try to get some sleep. The inferno is still inside my head and I choke back thoughts and fears. It is clear from the faces of other passengers that I am not the only one visiting Bali for the same reason. The plane arrives and I walk out as if in a dream, watching people in the packed departure lounges. They all know why we, forlorn ones, are getting off the plane and we know why they are getting on it – to get away from this paradise island which overnight has turned into a pocket of hell.

The airport corridors seem awfully long. Eventually I see a desk with a big sign saying 'Family Crisis Centre'. This must be where I go. A woman in long, wavy clothes sits me down and asks my name, who I am looking for and my country of origin. I go through passport control, another long queue, watching people around me. In hindsight I realise that many are journalists making their way to the hotspot.

I step over the yellow line to the man behind the desk. "How long will you be here?" he asks.

I look at him blankly. "I don't know, my brother was in the bomb" I say.

"Oh, sorry" he responds sadly and stamps the passport. I carry on and the wavy lady appears with another woman. "There are some people here to meet you." I had sent word to Mel so it was likely to be her. We walk along another long corridor and the lady puts her arm around my shoulder. "They are waiting at the end there; be warned it isn't good news".

I swallow and breath in and out. My mind spinning, I find myself standing in front of two strangers. The girl in shorts looks straight at me and says in a thick, Australian accent: "Totty?" I nod. It is Elissa and a man named Mike.

"They've found Jon, he's dead".

All I can muster is "How..?"

"They found his room key on him, we're pretty sure it's him".

Her arms wrap round me, as do the man's. I can't breathe. Everything feels so claustrophobic. I want to push them off and scream but all I can do is just keep breathing.

They seem to carry me all the way out of the building, across the road to a big yellow jeep. Two arms holding me up. We clamber into the back and they explain that we are going to the hotel; Jon's hotel. It won't be far. She makes conversation and holds my hand. She asks me about Jon.

"Did he like football?" It shocks me back into reality, I almost laugh.

"No." To a non-football family, it seems such an odd question.

Mike is a colleague of Mel's from the Chinese International School in Hong Kong. He is holidaying in Bali. Unassuming and gentle, he has arrived on Sunday and, on hearing the news, had come straight to Mel. Although I have never met him before, he becomes my guardian angel. Over the next few days he goes everywhere with me, supporting me, rephrasing information so I can take things in, asking questions when I can't get the words out and letting me use his mobile 'phone non-stop. A true guardian angel.

When we get to the hotel, we meet Pete and Enrica, two volunteer expats assisting the British Consulate. We sit in the foyer on big wicker chairs around a little coffee table. The sun has gone down and the darkness of the Balinese night has set in. Mel's father, Bruce, who has flown in from Australia, is also there. Mel gives me a hug, but looks lost and worn out. She shows me a picture of Shane and hands me Jon's passport.

What is happening to me is happening all over the island to the relatives who are arriving. Some go straight to the hospital, some straight to the morgue, others to the Australian or British Consulate, some, with no idea where to go, look for answers, look for loved ones, not knowing if they are dead or alive. Pete and Enrica want to take me to meet the British Consul.

"She's just got here guys, she's only just been told, give her a break." Elissa takes them aside to explain what information we have. My numbness starts to fade away and I suddenly click – things need to happen. How do we get him home? He must have insurance. Enrica offers to find out.

The hotel front desk asks me to come to the 'phone. It is Sean O'Maonaigh, Jon's Head Teacher. He has heard the news and wants to help in what ever way possible. Then Derek, Jon's friend and colleague, who he had flown as far as Singapore with, calls and wants to help. Then Dad calls, and I tell him that his oldest son is dead. He doesn't seem to take it in.

How do you tell someone their son is dead? How do you take it in, when it is 5000 miles away? I try to call Mum to break the news to her but she isn't in. She is none the wiser, busying herself with a series of lectures on 'The History and Culture of the Islamic World'. How ironic.

I decide to stay in Jon's room at the Hotel. Elissa shows me the way. Past the restaurant where Jon had his last meal, we follow the path he had walked up to his room in the far left corner of the quadrant of the hotel. It is a typical Balinese hotel with one storey around a courtyard filled with trees and stepping stones. Each room has its own entrance onto a balcony where lovers, families, travellers sit and listen to the grasshoppers in the night, with the murmur of the sea swelling up onto the shore as the sun sets, just like you see in all the brochures.

Jon's room is on the upper floor next to Mel's and Shane's, their balconies separated by shared stairs. Elissa shows me Jon's large bag. I open the zip: it is like opening up a mental picture of Jon. Everything means something, full of memories and all in blue. His blue Saigon T-shirt which he had worn most of last summer, his blue striped shirts and, as I delved more blue T-shirts all folded so neatly, his tennis racquet and ties, an *FHM* magazine and two books, both so apt: Graham Greene's *The Quiet American* and Ben Elton's *Dead Famous*.

I rummage, almost trying to find Jon, for it definitely smells of him, familiar Jonathan smell that lingers in his bedroom back in England even though he hasn't been in it for months, a typical bachelor smell of old clothes, new clothes, after-shave and beer all melded into his personal odour. I pick up his Saigon T-shirt and, yes, there is the smell, which will eventually be a distant memory.

We set off to the hospital with Pete and Enrica. Pete is a Kiwi married to an Indonesian and Enrica is from Britain. Both have lived in Bali for quite a while and speak good Bahasa. They became our escorts for the next week. Wherever we go one of them, if not both, are there. Like all the volunteers, they simply want to do something, anything, to help ease the aftermath of this atrocity. Along with 100 or so other expatriates, they sign up at the British Consulate to assist the staff in whatever way they can. Good people are not hard to find in times like these.

Pete drives a large people carrier which takes us down to the hospital. There is still much disarray where the bombs went off. The main road through the bomb-site is shut so Pete drives the long way round. I am completely disoriented. I have no idea where the bomb had gone off in relation to the hotel and I have no desire to go anywhere near.

The Sanglah Hospital is huge with long bungalow buildings for wards, all connected by covered walk ways, crawling with people. We struggle to find the entrance: it is a maze and there are so many cars around. Pete takes a left turn only to find us driving in the dark straight down a dead-end towards the morgue. Elissa, who had inadvertently walked into that area that morning, flips. "No, you can't go down there, don't go down there, turn around".

Pete thinks she is frightened of the guards with guns and says "You can't go around being frightened of people with guns, it won't get you any-where." He turns around and parks farther down the road.

We walk along the dark street to the hospital. The entrance is still unclear but we follow signs to the Crisis Centre. This takes us past the lists, hand written in black marker, of names with the words MISSING in bold at the top or INJURED. There is no official DEAD list as yet; you are presumed missing until identified. People stand helplessly in front of them, desperately trying to find information.

The Crisis Centre is up the stairs in a large hall, run by more volunteers, ex-pats, Balinese, friends and locals. Here there are more lists. The desks are laid out with helpers on one side and pockets of people searching on the other. There is some sort of system but it isn't consistent. One person asks you to sit down and give a description of the person you are looking for, distinguishing marks *etc*, only for the next person to ask again.

I explain to a volunteer that I know my brother is dead because his room key has been found and I really want to know how long it will be before he can be released. As there is no official dead list yet, she hasn't dealt with this question yet, so she goes away to ask what to do.

A short, balding man with a deep Yorkshire accent introduces himself as Mark Wilson, the British Honorary Consul. Thank goodness I think, at last someone who can tell me what to do. It soon transpires that the British Ambassador to Indonesia has been and gone, leaving Mr Wilson to deal with the aftermath. Apart from giving me his card, he can tell me little else than that there are 22 British missing with 11 confirmed dead. He has a piece of paper to jot names down on. So, once again, I tell the story of the key in the pocket. Mark Wilson adds Jon to his confirmed list, gives me his contact details and disappears.

Mel and Elissa have gone into the foyer while their father looks at the photos of the dead, still trying to find Shane. A woman asks me if I would like to look at them, but I see little point. Jon has already been identified. I hope that they have a system of numbers for the bodies, but this is a very grey area.

About 11.30pm Lee comes in and sits down next to me. Even though he is an American he has a Dutch air about him. He is tall, good-looking man and pleasant. I tell him my story and he sighs. Yes, he knows the body I am talking about, his friend Sam had found it. He immediately grabs his mobile and makes a call. "Hey, Sam, you still down in the morgue? You remember the guy with the key? I've got the sister here, she wants to talk to you". He passes the 'phone to me.

I pause while I try to think what to say. "I just want to ask what sort of condition the body is in? I just need to prepare myself for when I see him."

"Well, what can I say? The skin's first layer has been burnt off. He's like all the bodies down here, it's not good."

There isn't much else to say except "Thanks for finding him".

This quiet American has been in the morgue since Sunday, trying to help co-ordinate and identify some of the 200 bodies coming in. By going through every single body in detail, he and the other volunteers are searching for any means of identification. A watch, a necklace, a wedding ring, a wallet, which will distinguish one from another. He is one of the unsung heroes and always will be to our family. We can't bring Jon back but Sam's efforts means Jon has been positively identified. Sam, like the other morgue helpers, will live with those images for the rest of his life.

Lee points out that there will be no viewing now as the Australians are coming in tomorrow with their forensic teams and no one is going any-where until they have checked everyone. It is becoming clear to me that getting Jon home isn't going to be so easy. I go outside, where Pete offers me some food. The Crisis Centre has every kind of food imaginable for families of victims, from hamburgers to fruit, the Balinese community are providing for the bereaved. Unfortunately I have lost my appetite.

Bruce is sitting by the doorway, smoking and counselling the girls; he is a retired doctor and is trying to explain the patterns of grief. I sit down next to them and borrow Mike's 'phone to finally ring Mum. However, I don't have to break the news to her as someone has already 'phoned her to extend their sympathies, thinking that she already knows.

I've seen enough films so I knew what to do next. "Mum, you need to fax through Jon's dental records". I had already mentioned this before leav-ing Penang. Mum faxes them through to the Crisis Centre. The disap-pointment is overwhelming. When they come through they are very dark and indecipherable.

I ring England again and bark at Mum: "Mum, we can't read these, they are all black". I start to lose it.

"It's the best I can do", she says "they are written on old, brown card-board."

Jon had not been to the UK dentist for a while and his records had not been updated into the modern world of data disk filing.

"Well, you will have to go back and get them to re-write them" I demand.

I can sense Mum getting upset. Fortunately Natalie, my sister-in-law, is with her in Aldbury. She jumps in her car and heads straight to the dentists to get a fresh copy.

"Don't you think Tobias should come out" Mum asks again.

"No, I'll be fine."

"We can get him on a flight tonight (they are eight hours behind)".

"No, it'll be OK" I try to sound convincing but Mum knows better and arranges for Tobias to fly out.

There is nothing else we can do at the hospital. We make our way back to the hotel. Mel and her sister offer to stay with me but I just want to go to bed. Exhausted, I ring my husband in Penang but there is no answer. I lie on the bed and cry until I drop off to sleep, still holding Jon's blue Saigon t-shirt in my hand.

****

Brian and Janine in Vietnam wrote -

Not long ago Jon played a main role in rescuing a woman from the Saigon River. He made very little of what he had done. He was also the only person to stop cars in the city for people to cross over. Most people are afraid of the motorbikes.

Jon added something extra, positive and special to our life. His legacy to us will be to remember what is really important in life.

****

15th October

****

European Council of International Schools (ECIS) website.

*ECIS is deeply saddened to learn of the deaths of **Jonathan (Jon) Mark Ellwood** and **Miss Deborah Snodgrass** who lost their lives in the recent tragic events in Bali.*

***Jon Mark Ellwood**, an experienced international educator, was currently serving as a Director of Studies and Head of Humanities at the International School Ho Chi Minh City. Born in 1965, he was awarded a BA in History and German in 1987, a Post Graduate Certificate of Education in 1994 and a MA in Education in 1997. Upon earning his teacher qualification, he taught History and German at Ashlyns Secondary School in the UK from 1994-95. His career in international education began with his appointment as IGCSE Co-ordinator and History teacher at Antwerp International School from 1995-96. In 1998 he was appointed to Bavarian International School in Germany where he served as Humanities Department Head, Careers Advisor and Theory of Knowledge co-ordinator. This was immediately followed by his appointment in 2001 to the International School of Ho Chi Minh City, where Jon played an integral role in many aspects of school development and improvement.*

Jon is survived by his mother, Caroline Ellwood, current editor of the ECIS International School Magazine, and frequent presenter at ECIS conferences, father Peter a UN worker and his brother, Tobias and sister, Totty.

*Among the many still missing in Bali are international educators, **Shane Walsh-Till** from the Chinese International school and **Jamie Wellington** from Jakarta International School.*

Students and colleagues throughout the world of international education will greatly miss them.

****

The Melasti Beach Bungalows Hotel is on the beach, but when I look out of my window in the morning it looks as if I have stumbled on a graveyard. The beach area directly adjacent to the balcony is closed off by a large wall and looks as if it is used regularly for Hindu rituals. This involves the burning of incense and piles of wood. Burnt stakes are scattered all over the area and it is not a welcome sight. It really looks like a crematorium so I quickly shut the curtain and take in my room.

It is a fairly spartan L-shaped room with a double bed covered with a large red velvet quilt. I sit on the bed and try to call Matt. He is amidst the usual breakfast frenzy and school rush so we can't talk for long. Talking to Felicity first just makes me cry. So far removed from reality, her innocent voice comes on the 'phone:

"Are you looking after Jonathan?"

"Yes, I am trying to" I reply. Matt comes to the 'phone and I well up: "Oh, Matt it's Jonathan, it's my Jonathan."

"I know Totty, I know, I'm so sorry."

That is it, there is nothing else to say, I just sob it over and over again. "My Jonathan's gone".

I 'phone Dad in Vienna but he is asleep, so I try Mum, who is now sleeping by the 'phone in the living-room in Aldbury. It is the middle of the night for her so there is not much to add except that she has booked Tobias' flight and he is bringing the freshly-copied dental records. Part of me feels a failure for needing Tobias, the other part feels relief. If necessary he can identify Jon.

I go out onto the balcony at about 7.30am. The sun has risen and the Balinese island is awakening to me for the first time. Green trees, a view out to the sea and Balinese architecture all around. Mel is on the other balcony and I suddenly feel very shy, as if I am invading her world. I have been so caught up in Jon that I haven't really understood Mel's pain of losing a husband. Mel and Shane are truly international people. They met in Australia but then spent their lives and careers travelling, building a nest in each new country, working as a team in the same school. International schools like to employ couples and here is a particularly employable couple. Mel, the PE teacher and Shane the Head of Middle School, both dedicated to their work and with a keen sense of humour.

I go over to ask how she is. She is writing again in her note-book. She always seems to be writing. Here is a person I barely knew and suddenly we are bound for life it seems.

"Would you mind writing down something about what Jonathan was doing on his last day?"

"Of course not..." The barriers are lifted. She smiles and starts to chat about "Jonny" and her eyes glisten. She is still living in hope that Shane might be alive.

I breakfast with Mike Etheridge. We sit by the pool and ponder the day before us. He calmly puts up with my yapping. I feel an overwhelming need to talk about Jon. Mike had never met him but listens intently.

It is Tuesday and we arrange for Mel's dad to visit the morgue and try to find Shane. He will also look for Jon. I show him a number of photos and rattle off all the details that might help. I can't remember what sort of watch he had, but I know it was on his right hand. He also had a scar from surgery at the base of his back. Mel confirms this as she had worked at the Bavarian school with Jon, when she endured his back traumas which resulted in an operation. Bruce takes a passport photo I have found in Jon's travel wallet and a large A4 picture of Shane. He is confident that he will recognise Shane as he had been at their wedding. "Don't worry Babe, I'll find him" he tells Mel, and he goes with Pete.

Pete is a bit of a mystery; he is a short New Zealand chap who looks as if he has been through a war. His face is quite scarred and he keeps himself very quiet. He mutters comments like: "I've seen worse than this" and is quite resilient to the whole situation. He has clearly served in some army but none of us can work out which one. Currently, he seems to be serving us and his loyalty to our group remains unbroken throughout the week.

We hear that there is to be an Australian briefing at 10am at the Hard Rock Café Hotel. We pile into a taxi and go the long route to the hotel, which is in fact round the corner. No building in Bali is allowed to be built higher than a coconut tree, but The Hard Rock Café obviously has a warped idea of the height of coconut trees. It is more like a palace than a hotel. With a large drive up a hill to the entrance, it feels very safe. Security has been heightened: not only are the Australians using it for their briefing but the press have descended on it and, as we discover later, are also using it as their base.

Whilst getting out of the taxi the enormity of grief starts to hit me. Families, groups of people and individuals slowly walk towards the Hotel. Mel runs towards a man she had seen at the hospital. He looks worn out, he has clearly been crying all night. He has come to Bali to find his Mother and 13-year old-sister, which he has had no luck in doing.

We follow the crowd down the massive Corridors of Fame, passing famous names and faces that on another occasion might have been interesting. A sign points the way up the stairs to another carpeted corridor, this time full of press, harvesting pictures of the bereaved, and on into a large conference room. At the front is a long table for the various Australian officials and rows and rows of chairs which are slowly filled by the bereaved.

Just sitting there makes me realise once again that it is not just me. This is a tragedy beyond a scale I can conceive. Mothers, fathers, brothers, uncles, aunts and friends: all looking for somebody to help them find their loved ones. The room is very quiet, despite so many people, but heavy with anxiety. Some are crying quietly, others whisper consolation. Many are still in shock and wait numbly for some sort of information.

I suddenly have an overwhelming need to leave this awful room full of sorrow. I get up and stagger to the nearby toilet. Sitting in the cubicle I find the privacy I need. I then let go. I start to cry. I howl and then I retch. It hurts. All I can do is cry and remind myself that I can't bring him back.

After what seems like forever I come out and wash my face. Somehow it is important to remain composed. I look in the mirror, take a deep breath and return to the briefing. Everyone is still waiting. The Australian officials are stuck in traffic due to the heightened security. A lady stands up and asks for the press to leave. They are all lined up on the side of the room, taking pictures of unhappy people. So they leave and hover outside instead.

The Australian Consul arrives and apologises profusely. He is a gentle man, with blonde hair and a gallant air about him. In his deep Australian accent he explains what is going to happen. "We are going to give you as much information as we have. To be honest the agenda for this meeting was put together on a scrap of paper on the way here in a taxi. We are working night and day to deal with this situation as best we can." He then introduces the team standing next to him. Names fly by: from right to left there are a doctor with experience in pathology, an Australian Army Colonel from the team who flew in on Saturday night, a psychiatrist/social worker and the Australian Consul himself.

The Consul explains what the Australians have been doing. They have clearly been working hard and their main priority is to get the critically injured out of Bali. They are very concerned that there are still injured out there who have not gone to hospital and therefore have not been accounted for. After he finishes he hands over to the Army man who explains the security measures. Finally the doctor goes through the issues of identifying bodies. He predicts that it could take up to four months, and paints quite a grim picture. Meanwhile everyone is getting a bit twitchy. They have come here for information about where to go from here but are just getting facts about what has happened so far.

The Consul opens discussion to the floor and it becomes like an Alcoholics Anonymous meeting. It is dreadful. One by one people are standing up and explaining who they have lost.

"Hello, I'm looking for my brother."

"I know my wife and her best friend are dead."

"I'm looking for my son."

"I'm looking for my husband but don't know what to do."

However, like most public meetings, it takes one strong outburst to really express how everyone truly feels. A voice from the back says "Hi, my name's Mark and I'm British, I'm looking for my girl-friend. I'm pretty sure she's dead and what I want to know is where is my fucking Government?"

Everyone turns round to see a young man holding up a lost person's paper he has created with his girlfriend's picture on it.

"I know this might not be the right place to say this but there is no where else for me to go. My Government has done nothing so far, they are not interested, I can't get through to the Honorary British Consul and I have had to do everything myself. I have searched through all the hospitals and I've been to the morgue."

The Australian Consul tries to treat it diplomatically and offers any Australian help he can but the young man will have none of it.

"What is going on here? There is no central help, nobody knows what is going on, nobody knows where to go. You go to the Crisis Centre and they say one thing and here you say another." Tears are falling as he speaks. Mark's painful outcry opens the floodgates for many of the bereaved. One by one they stand up to complain about the lack of support.

A rugby tournament had been taking place in Bali and many rugby players were either in Paddy's Bar or the Sari Club. Behind me a huge, broad-shouldered rugby player stands up. "I have lost my wife and my son is critically injured and has been airlifted to Australia. I don't know where and can't seem to find a 'phone number which doesn't put me on hold, or can give me information. In the meantime why can't I identify my wife, she has a fake hip, surely that's not too hard to find."

The doctor answers this one: "Distinguishing marks are very important but due to the burns many are not recognisable."

Somehow it all washes over me. I seem to be at a different stage to the rest; in my mind I have Jonathan's body already. I am not looking anymore and have the confirmation which everyone else is dreading or waiting to hear.

The questions go on and on and more and more people demand a help line, in some ways telling the Australians what they think should be done. A central point is missing. Lee, the American from The Crisis Centre is there too. He tries to explain the function of the Centre. The Australians want everyone to go through the Consul and not through The Crisis Centre which was set up by volunteers and is not official.

Somebody shouts out "So you mean that whole process we went through at the hospital, of writing out forms to identify our loved ones, was a waste of time."

"You need to fill in a form at the Consulate which will then allow us to pursue your case."

People are livid. "Excuse me, why can't you get the forms from the hospital and use them?"

"The Indonesians have now taken those forms and locked them up. We need to be careful here and not step on the Indonesians toes, it is their country and we cannot take over their system."

"Surely you could at least photocopy them?" someone shouts.

It is doing everyone's head in and makes me realise that, as a British citizen, I am in the wrong place. If the Australians are filling in their own forms I need to be filling in a form at my Consulate, wherever that may be. I put this to the Australian panel and they agree that I need to go to my own Consulate. In my mind the ball seems to be rolling again but I can't actually do anything yet. People are getting very heated and the Australian Consul, who has been up since midnight Saturday, is starting to look uncomfortable and frazzled. He abruptly calls the meeting to a close and reminds everyone that there will be a briefing (on a bereaved person's suggestion) at the Hard Rock Hotel every day.

I go in search of Mark, the Brit who had complained so effectively. He seems to be the only other UK citizen here, but he has reached a point of complete distress, and decided to go to the media. He has arranged to speak on ITV. He wants me to talk to them with him. He was getting quite upset so I tell him to sit down and write out his thoughts. He scribbles down a quite vindictive statement.

It is becoming clear that his anger, although justified, isn't something I can be part of right now. I am not ready to share my grief on national television and it doesn't feel right. I have found Jon; anything else seems immaterial. I feel numb. Mark presented another dimension to the whole awful event: the UK interest in the bomb and the aftermath.

We return to our hotel across town, next door to which there is a restaurant, Café Barney's, which sells pizza. Most westerners who were not involved in the tragedy have left Bali and the waitresses now outnumber the guests. We seat ourselves in the corner by a fountain. Mel continues to tell funny 'Jonny' stories from when they lived in Bavaria.

"He used to live one stop after us on the train. After a night out he would fall asleep on the train and wake up at the end stop, or even go to the end and back to the beginning!"

She seems to be resigning herself to the knowledge that Shane is dead. She talks about having him cremated, as that is what he said he wanted. Her problem is that they didn't have a hometown. They had married and left Australia and were international citizens with no permanent base. Apparently Shane had always said he wanted his ashes spread on the Sydney cricket pitch, where he and Jon were due to go this Christmas. It seems a lovely idea but Mel is unsure if Shane's mother will approve. It is a tricky one; as his wife of six years Mel obviously feels that Shane's ashes should be at her disposal. Having children myself I can understand the other perspective: you would want your child nearby. Jonathan has no wife so we will of course bury him in our village church in Aldbury.

The conversation obviously hurts Mel a lot. She gets out her Walkman, turns it on and listens to her and Shane's song, probably for the hundredth time. She is always listening and writing in her notepad. She is so gracious though, like a swan in sorrow, always looking beautiful and yet pained by the acute circumstances. Elissa frequently holds her hand and asks is she is OK. Elissa and Mike are constantly smoking and it makes me think of Jon giving up smoking. Jon started smoking when he was at Oxford Poly (sorry Jon, Oxford Brookes) and I ranted at him about it for years. He always said he would stop eventually. Then one day, aged 35, he stopped. He went on a ski-course, probably the hardest place to stop, surrounded by pit stops and beer. He just woke up one morning and gave up. The funny thing was he didn't tell anyone, quite typical Jon really. He came back to the UK and it took me a few weeks to work out what was different. I was very proud.

After the pizza, which none of us really eat, Mike and I try to organise a ticket back to the UK for me. We walk up the road when Mike, who decides a Baskin Robbins ice cream is the comfort food he needs right now, asks someone where to find a travel agent. It turns out Café Barney's has one hidden behind the restaurant. We return to find a bizarre set-up. The office for the travel agent is a table at the side of a Christian hall. At one end is a big cross and about 50 chairs; to the side are a lot of tables and to our left the travel agents: a large desk with filing cabinets and a computer. The chap is terribly friendly and does his best to help, but it all seems unclear as I don't know how long Tobias will be here. We may be able to leave straight away if he identifies Jon the day he arrives. Pretty naïve of me really to even think that.

We return to the pool in the hotel, which only yesterday seemed such a foreign place. All the staff wear lovely green Balinese outfits, the men with pretty head wraps and many with wraparounds instead of trousers. Everybody smiles at you and gives you that sorrowful look. They all know. As we pass reception the manager comes to express his sorrow.

The sisters soon retire and by the time I have had my refreshing dip, Mike is fast asleep in the chair. His 'phone rings. We get the news that another teacher, Jamie Wellington from Jakarta, the son of a science teacher at Mike's school, was also lost in the blast. Mike goes to tell Mel and, just as I am ordering my drink, Bruce, and Pete the Kiwi expat arrive. They have spent the whole day at the morgue and both need a beer. They waited all morning to be allowed to see the bodies. They searched everywhere but couldn't find Shane.

Bruce thinks that the body that is supposed to be Jon is definitely not Jon. He says the body does not look like the photo at all. And the body with the room key has no scar on his stomach. My heart sinks. Maybe the room key is not enough to identify him? Maybe it belonged to someone else? I am also confused as I thought the scar was on his back. I console myself knowing that Tobias would soon be here to sort it out. He will recognise Jonathan.

Poor Bruce is in a sad state. He keeps shaking his head and saying how appalling the facilities are at the morgue, that he has never seen anything like it: body bags lying in the sun everywhere with only melting blocks of ice to keep them cool. There seems to be no consistency, no clear number system. It is too big a scale of crisis for the Balinese to deal with. He is so horrified and disgusted by it all he plans to talk to ABC – Australian radio – that evening. He recommends that Mel should give up the search. "I'm afraid you will not get closure here, you will have to find some other way of finding it. It is going to take a very long time for them to go through all those bodies and identify them."

He is angered and distraught by the day's experience. It reminds me of the young British man this morning at the briefing, who also reached the point when enough was enough and talking to the media seemed the only way of getting the message across.

We discuss the plan for tomorrow. My guardian angel, Mike joins us, still there taking it all in, sitting next to me. Pete looks exhausted. He has been helping non-stop since Sunday, ferrying bereaved families back and forth across town and today looking through the bodies. He is white as a sheet. He has hardly been home except to sleep, and not much of that as his young daughter is ill with a cold.

He explains that the body that they think is Jon's is now in a refrigerated container. It appears the British are the only ones to have a fridge container. Bizarrely, I am quite elated by this news. Jon is being recognised as a British citizen and things seem to be happening. In his army manner Pete goes through our itinerary. I am expecting Tobias to arrive tonight, so first thing tomorrow we can go to the British Consulate. It seems the Consulate is now clued up on Jon's case and once we've been there we would go to the morgue to identify him. Some British officials are being flown in and Jon, plus another British body, are a priority. For the first time someone is taking our case seriously. Meanwhile Mel, Elissa and Bruce will go to the other side of the island to pick up their air-tickets and then fly, after lunch, to Perth. Mike offers to stay with me in Bali to make sure I am alright. Whilst discussing all this the 'phone rings: it is Dad wanting news. Then Sean O'Maonaigh, Jon's Head at his school, calls with news of Jon's insurance cover.

It is now after 8pm. The sun goes down quickly in south-east Asia. In the centre of the tropical garden is a patio and Mike and I sit down for a beer. Mel has gone to bed, exhausted. Her father, is about to be interviewed on his balcony by the Australian broadcasting man and says that once he has done the interview they will all get out of Bali as soon as possible. He is going to criticise the system and expects that they will not be welcome by the Indonesians any more and it would be safer to return to Australia. They change their flights by 'phone in order to be on the first plane out. This is a simple task as Quantas have put on extra planes.

So we sit and have some beers. Mum rings to tell me that Tobias is sitting in a hotel in Singapore. His flight has been delayed leaving Heathrow for security reasons (it turned out a pram was unaccounted for) and wouldn't arrive until tomorrow morning. My heart sinks.

The 'phone rings again and this time it is Pikos, my school friend from Atlantic College (Wales). Pikos always turns up in my life at the most odd times and I rely on this to maintain our contact. We never call each other or arrange to meet. We just seem to bump into one another from time to time, catch up, put the world to rights, have a good meal, until the next time. So out of all the people in the world to call me on Mike's 'phone it is totally appropriate. I leave the group to sit by the wall and chat, looking out at the dark beach and the tide creeping in. Pikos had opened *The Independent* this morning and seen Jon's picture. I have known Pikos since I was 16. He came to my wedding and knows the entire Ellwood family well. He always shows a fond admiration for what we all get up to, and he does not beat about the bush. He wants to know how I am and how my family are coping. His familiar voice, calling all the way from London, sends me a message of support and concern.

We discuss the bomb. He has a friend who lost someone in 9/11 so he is probably more aware of that tragedy than I am. I had watched it on television in disbelief. I even watched the memorial service a month later and had been touched by Sigorney Weaver's words:

'Have you lost someone? We are sorry for your loss.
Do you know someone who has lost someone. We are sorry.
Do you know someone whose family have lost someone. We are sorry' and so on.

It touched me at the time. 9/11 was on such a large scale that there clearly were so many people who, even if not directly, knew someone who had been affected by the attack. Now my life is part of an attack. A vicious bomb has killed my Jonathan. It is still too much to take in.

I return to the pergola where Elissa has joined Mike and another round of beer is ordered. Elissa tells me how they spent the Sunday looking for Shane and Jon in the hospital. All she could think of was 'we must not forget to ask about Jon'.

She is worried that in the frenzy of looking for Shane they would forget Jon, so everywhere they went she kept saying the name over and over again. Bruce joins us and more cigarettes are smoked. It is amazing how many they all go through. Bruce never stops talking. He is full of stories of his wives, his yacht, his home. Suddenly Elissa interrupts him and says: "Dad, do you mind, can we have some quiet."

"Of course babe, of course I understand."

Bruce takes his daughter's rebuff well and pulls out another cigarette. Two minutes later he starts telling us another story.

By 10pm I have had enough too. I take my leave and go upstairs to the room to 'phone Matt, but he's not there, so I call Dad in Vienna. It feels as if I am calling Mum and Dad separately at least four times a day. Aldbury, Vienna, then Aldbury. The only problem is I can never remember what I have said to whom.

16th October

Jonathan is a typical Ellwood: ambitious, a good organiser and with a fervour for life.

We all have it and our parents have brought us up to believe that we can achieve anything if we want to. Born only one year apart, for the first eight years Tobias and Jon did everything together. Mum even dressed them the same. So one of them was bound to rebel. It happened quite naturally though: as puberty arrived Jon developed severe acne and Tobias just had a spot or two. Jon became a greasy, long-haired 70's teenager and Tobias became a pure-bred Eagle Scout. Jon broke the ground for us children by having the first girl-friend, but it was Tobias who had the long-term relationship and talked to Mum about it. Jonathan's spots disappeared but the scars remained. He was a reserved young man, who retired into his shell and he would wait until people approached him rather than force himself on a situation, a characteristic which enabled him to be a very good listener as well as a trusted mentor for many students. Tobias, on the other hand, became taller and more out-going. From Eagle Scout to Chairman of the Loughborough Student's Union to a Captain in the Royal Green Jackets, he was a confident leader with fire and ambition. As with many families, the brothers would meet up at reunions but the true contact with each other was through myself, who appreciated qualities in both and saw beyond their bickering over who had stolen the drill, the CD player or the tennis racquet.

Jon was a catch as far as woman were concerned, blonde, Cheshire cat smile and pleasant. He was also quite selective and had become a confirmed bachelor. However at 37 he was starting to see that flirtations and independence was not the be-all and end-all. He was thinking about finding that important someone and could see the benefits of a family. He was very fond of my two children and now that his close friends had all procreated, it was definitely time to settle down…

****

We were so shocked to hear of Jon's tragic death last week. It is never easy coming to terms with the loss of someone close to you, but to have the appalling trauma of his death played out on the world stage must have added to your sense of grief and loss. We are so sorry. It has doubtless been an immensely difficult time for you all.

Jon was a talented man in his prime. His abilities as a director, teacher, organiser, ICT specialist, curriculum planner, singer, beer drinker and loyal friend were second to none. His easy-going manner endeared him to a great many people.

But as a close friend, who always kept in touch, however far away he was, who remembered birthdays, arrived over the Christmas period with a present every year and had such a kind heart and generous spirit, we shall miss him enormously.

As you may know, I saw Jon at Heathrow just before his return to Vietnam. He seemed really well, was planning a career as a singer (!!) and was clearly thriving in the international school environment he knew so well. He was full of anticipation for the future. It was just a matter of time before he became a Headteacher.

It is so hard to come to terms with his death in that context. We can only dream of what might have been, but his presence is still very much with us, his hearty laugh after a few beers, his warmth and his kindness; all the qualities that made him such a good friend. It has been so hard to put into words what his loss means. The pain and the agony you must all be feeling cannot be imagined.

We talked the other day of how we had always anticipated Jon being there into old age. We have so many good memories of him and tragically it is now these we must take with us.

Richard (one of Jon's closest friends)

****

Tobias is 6 foot 3in tall, a large man who doesn't get comfortable in a small confined seat. After two hauls of economy travel he is certainly ready to get off the plane. It is grim on the aircraft, with only about six passengers on board, all looking sorrowful; all no doubt, arriving at Denpasar Airport, Bali, for the same reason.

I wait with Mike outside the airport. We are amazed at how empty it is. Large, empty spaces, normally heaving with passengers, replaced by silence and a few cleaners walking about. No-one is travelling. We stand next to the railing while sporadically people make their way through the sliding doors. Mike asks me if Tobias looks like Jonathan, "No, he looks like me" I reply and I realise that I am now waiting for my only brother.

You take it for granted that you are one of three. Your sibling rivalry, your connection within the family, it is all part of the course. My two pillars; I had always had Jonathan on one side of my life and Tobias on the other. As Tobias said later: "Now we'll always be known as Tobias and Totty, who lost their brother in the Bali bomb."

My brother strolls through the sliding doors, a laptop bag in one hand, a small hold-all in the other; I run up and give him a big hug, there is a sense of 'Ellwood' about him which feels like home.

Once again I am walking to the yellow Jeep, but it is with a lighter step as the weight is being shared now. We drive back to the Melasti Beach Bungalows where Mel, Elissa and Bruce are getting ready to leave. In the alleyway, Bruce briefs Tobias on what to expect. He is still convinced it isn't Jon.

We say our farewells, hug and cry. Saying goodbye to Mel is quite odd. Through death I made a friend for life. She will always be the last person who saw and appreciated Jon.

We drive to the British Consulate. It feels as though we are crossing the entire island. In fact, we only travel about 20 minutes, across town. In typical south-east Asian style we take a short-cut which bounces us through a car park.

Enrica, our other expat volunteer, is English but has married an Australian. She has briefly worked at Bali International School and has two small children, like me. She is feeling very shaken as she has just discovered that a good friend of hers, Debbie Snodgrass from the Bali International School, is also missing. However, she is keen to help us. She explains about the consulates in Bali.

"There are some real consulates, like the Australian one, but most are small, honorary consulates which run alongside the Consul's business. In the British case it is a pub called the Cat and Fiddle." Tobias and I are stunned. The British Consulate is based at a pub! We laugh, not realising that it is about to get even odder.

The Cat and Fiddle is down a back lane on the north-west side of town. Like most English pubs it has a big sign outside with a picture of a cat and fiddle. As with most eating establishments in south-east Asia, the seating is outside with a covered area over the bar. On the menu are fish and chips and a full English breakfast. At the back a small office, on the door of which is a sign that reads 'British Consul Bali.' It is the place to come if you are British and need a birth, marriage or, in our case, death certificate. I remember hearing that Mick Jagger and Jerry Hall had a Hindu wedding in Bali; obviously they hadn't come to our man in Bali, as their marriage wasn't apparently recognised once they tried to get divorced.

Today Mark, our man in Bali, is very busy indeed. He has a team of volunteers scurrying around the restaurant. They are all very friendly but I couldn't help feeling that they have wandered in for a steak and kidney pie, realised the officials are a bit short staffed and offered to help. He, his almost identical brother, and their team are working all hours to cope with this disaster.

Tobias, Mike, Enrica and I wander in and sit at a table waiting for some attention. We wait for a long time and eventually a large, motherly lady in her late thirties sits down very efficiently at the head of the table and introduces herself. In her most sympathetic, softened voice she says "Hello, I'm the Family Liaison Officer from the Anti-terrorist Squad."

A young, tall, blonde man sits down next to her. He is from London Scotland Yard, one of the police officers here to help. It was obvious they have both recently arrived for their attire is clearly suited for colder climates and they were both sweating underneath their heavy clothing.

"We understand that your brother has been positively IDd" she says, so quietly that we have to lean towards her to hear.

"So, we..." I lean further forward but I can't hear a word she was saying.

"So we are now waiting..." It is appalling. Here is somebody supposedly giving us important information, but she is so involved in breaking the news to us gently that we can't make head or tail of it. Tobias gets impatient.

"I hear what you are saying (just), but what is stopping us from going to the morgue now. That is where my brother is. That is where I want to go."

"We can't go to the morgue without a certain person who has access at the morgue" she starts to drift off.

"When will he be back?"

"I don't know."

"Well, I want to go to the morgue now, I've got my brother's dental records and, as it happens, his finger prints'. Jon had been falsely arrest-

With Tobias and Jon on my first day at school

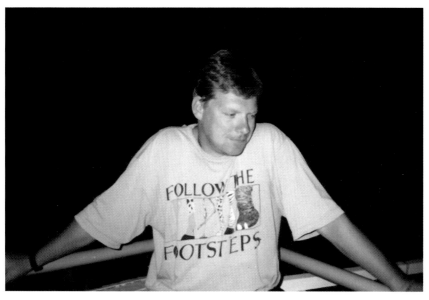

My brother, Jonathan

Jon

Jon with his homeroom students
at The Bavarian International School

Jon at the Valiant Trooper in Aldbury

The morgue showing the left container where Jon's body lay

*Three days after the bomb, a Balinese choir sings outside
the wreckage of the Sari Club and Paddy's Bar*

Peter Harvey, The Australian Air Force Padre at the morgue –
me in the background discussing the next move

The British Consulate in Bali – The Cat and Fiddle

Yet another delay... Consulting with Tobias in the morgue compound

The coffin leaves the church
Photo courtesy of John O'Reilly

The funeral: Tobias, Mum, me and Dad
Photo courtesy of John O'Reilly

6 months later... spring flowers on Jon's grave

ed after being suspected of being 'The Elusive Fox', a dodgy man who terrorised women in the Aldbury area in the 80's. Jon insisted on keeping and mounting in a frame the finger prints that has been taken. These were now in Tobias' folder.

"I can tell you now, that you won't be able to use the fingerprints".

"Why not" asked the Scotland Yard officer.

"Because they have to be verified by the person who took them, who isn't here now."

"Well, OK we've got the dental records, let's go" retorts Tobias.

"It's not that easy, we have to respect the system at the morgue and there is only one gentleman who so far can get in to see the bodies."

Tobias starts to get quite irate. "Then call this man and find out when we can get there."

"I'm not sure if we have a number." The Scotland Yard officer goes off to find out.

The Family Liaison Officer tries the hush-hush approach again. She cannot understand that we were not touchy-feely-kind-of-people. "We are doing our best to get you there as fast as possible. But another family are visiting the morgue so we must wait."

"Then let's go and wait outside the morgue" Tobias stands up, the Family Liaison Officer or 'Mrs Fluffy' as Tobias proceeds to call her, takes her opportunity to retreat and regroup with her official colleagues on another table. Tobias is beginning to feel let down.

Tobias goes outside and discovers the press waiting for him. It is the BBC with Clive Myrie, asking what is going on. Tobias recognises Clive from his days serving in Bosnia and lets rip. "This is a mess, there seems to be no organisation or communication. Where is the Foreign Office, where is the British Land Rover, where is the man in the Panama hat explaining to us what is going on?"

Tobias decides that we should make our own way to the morgue. Mrs Fluffy realises he is not going to change his mind. So the two-Jeep convoy heads across the island led by Pete. I make small talk with Flipper, as we nickname the Scotland Yard man. Mrs Fluffy stays behind. I ask Flipper if he has done this sort of thing before. "No, er... yes, well, not on this scale". He does not inspire confidence but he is all we have at the moment.

We arrive at Sanglah Hospital, this time in broad daylight. Tobias gazes in amazement at the chaos that I witnessed yesterday. The lists and lists of names of wounded and missing have grown – Jon's name, of course no longer there, but now on a confirmed dead list. The morgue is situated on the far side of the hospital. So we walk down the long, covered foot-ways, wards to either side with the injured and masses of people attending, visiting, sitting around. Policeman are chatting on every corner. We eventually come to a gap in a wall, which is surrounded by Army guards. A quick explanation as to why we are there and we are let through into the main court yard of the morgue itself.

The morgue consists of a small building of offices and slab rooms, a refrigerated room for ten bodies, a large car park area with a barn like covered space and a small open air temple. It has its own road entrance, but this is now closed and used by the military to house the tents for the guards. Normally a quiet place with only a handful of workers, today it has over 200 people rushing about the rows of body bags, many still baking in the sun. The chaos is as shocking as the stench. There are huge lorries in the middle of the car park, creating a protective shield between the morgue and the volunteers who all sit underneath the open 'barn'. Makeshift ply board coffins are stacked everywhere.

There are rows of tables with volunteers representing different nations on one side, bereaved on the other, with heated conversations between the two. There are more lists on any flat surface or wall. Chairs must be hard to come by as so many people are using up-turned coffins as benches. We can not immediately see the British desk (we were looking for a flag) so we walk straight to what seems to be the centre point of information.

Almost everyone has a mask on. A tall, robust, well-spoken gentleman walks up to us and with authority asks "Are you Mr Ellwood?" Taking off his mask he shakes hands with Tobias. Four words spoken, but said in such a way, that it inspires confidence and authority. "My name is David Magson."

There is another man with him, who really could have been our man in Bali. He looks like the archetypal colonial Brit, white empire building shorts, white shirt and grey hair. He is introduced as Calvin, but it could have been David Niven. Tobias assumes that David Magson is a doctor. David gets straight to business: "Your brother is in here, are you ready to come and look at him?"

Tobias is surprised, after Mrs Fluffy's peptalk we had anticipated a lengthy wait. This is good news.

"Yes, of course, where do we go?"

Tobias had seen a few mutilated bodies in his time in the army and has learnt to erase the images from his consciousness. Seeing your brother is a much more difficult experience. There was no question in his mind that he would identify Jonathan. Before he went in he said "when I come out, give me a moment."

I am offered a seat under a sheltered area while Tobias, now wearing a mask and rubber gloves, and shadowed by Flipper, follows David to the smaller of the refrigerated containers, which have been donated by a friend of the Honorary Consul who runs a delicatessen.

The Indonesian helpers open the large door and in the darkness Tobias can only see one large, dark body bag at the back. Tobias jumps in, pulling the bag apart but he cannot see very well. He asks David to help him move the body. "Er, no I'm sorry..." Tobias suddenly realises that David is not a doctor but only a volunteer and this is as far as this volunteer can go.

Tobias stares at the face for a full two minutes, taking in every feature. The body is covered in soot and clothing has been singed to the skin. The face is very puffy but it does look like Jon. They step out and Tobias returns to me. "Yes, it's him, I'm 90% sure. His nails, he had short chubby fingers with short, short nails?" Tobias is grasping for information. "Yes, he did. I remember he used to bite them."

Tobias asks for the body to be taken out of the container truck so he can turn it over in order to identify the scar from the back operation. The helpers take body number 157 through the main building, past the pathetic lines of coloured bags surrounded by ice and steaming in the heat, into a small court yard to the only bit of free space available. Tobias shows them how to roll Jonathan over to look for the scar. While they stand watching him, he grabs a rag and cleans the soot off Jon's back. He finds the two inch scar. Tobias is now 100 % certain that this is his brother. They zip the body bag up and he returns to me.

"It's Jon" he says and then walks off to the temple area to the left of the morgue. I watch him with pride and pity. I want to console him but this is an inconsolable moment. Tobias now has an image in his head that will remain with him for the rest of his life.

Tobias walks back up to me and I say "I want to go in."

"Are you sure?"

"Yes, definitely, I want to see him, not see him directly but see him in the bag and say goodbye."

So Tobias fits me out with a hat and gloves and takes my hand. We walk back in together. "Just keep your eyes on the floor, don't look around you." So I do that. As I walk through the first room all I can see are the ends of black and yellow and orange body bags, water on the floor and large, melting ice cubes. The smell of antiseptic overwhelms me. We carry on and arrive in the open area, walking past more bags. About three quarters of the way I look up and there in the middle of the path lies a large long, black, thick body bag.

The reality of it all sweeps over me and I just want to hug Jon. I kneel down and wrap my arms around this enormous black bag. It is cold, thick, plastic but I can feel Jon's enormous body inside and, for the first time in my life, I feel death.

Over and over again I weep "I'm sorry Jonathan, I'm so sorry", with my head resting on his I find myself speaking to him.

"It's alright now, we've found you and we're going to take you home, home to Aldbury where Mum is waiting for you." It is so, so awful.

Tobias puts his hand on Jonathan's arm. "Goodbye Jon, God bless."

And that is the last time I speak to Jonathan.

We make our way out. By this time the masses of bodies around mean nothing. We walk numbly through the aftermath of the atrocity. Lines and lines of black bags with numbers on them, the ice blocks struggling to keep them cold in the blazing sun and sweltering heat, all those dead people, lying on the paths, lying on the ground, awaiting attention.

Tobias's main reason for viewing Jonathan was not simply the identification. He also wanted to know how Jonathan had died, more importantly to see if he had had a prolonged death. This is an issue that every relative and friend of the dead would wonder and fret about. According to Tobias and the forensics who later examined him, they were pretty sure that he had died instantly. Something had gone straight through his chest. Although quite burnt he had had an instant impact with part of the bomb. I like to think that he was drinking his beer, heard a bang, saw a flash and that was it. Of course you go over and over it in your mind. We don't really know where he was, but it would have been instant. Others were not so fortunate, which is why the identification process for so many victims was to be arduous, painful and prolonged.

We return to the Consulate to sign a statement claiming that it is Jon and how Tobias has identified him. As Tobias walks along the corridors he tries to absorb some of what is happening in the Sanglah Hospital. "Can we go up to The Crisis Room?" he asks. We agree to meet Flipper back at the Cat and Fiddle.

We enter the large room where, as before, there are heaps of food on tables and distressed people looking for their loved ones. Someone tries to approach us to help, but we soon explain that in fact we are at the next stage.

Tobias starts acting quite strangely. He explained afterwards that he was desperately trying to get the image of the mutilated Jonathan out of his mind. He tries to eat something, looks at a different environment, anything to distract him from the distressing picture imprinted in his mind. We do not stay long.

Back at the Cat and Fiddle we try to determine our next step, the post mortem. I take the opportunity of a respite and call Mum and then Dad to tell them the news.

"It is Jon. Tobias was just brilliant, it seems the worst is over, we can start to organise bringing him home."

"When do you think the funeral will be?" Dad asks.

"I don't know, I think you had better check with Mum."

"OK I'll call her."

We find ourselves sitting at the Cat and Fiddle once again waiting for an official Consulate person to help us. Tobias signs a statement identifying Jon and we presume, rather foolishly, that that will be enough.

A Consulate man from Jakarta sits down and introduces himself as Ian. Once again we are forced to explain our situation, and that we need to move towards repatriation. Ian is not in a hurry "Well, first we will need to do a full post mortem."

Tobias starts to see red. "I'm sorry, but you don't need to do a full post mortem. I have identified my brother and now we need to get him out.

Nobody is slicing my brother up to do a full post mortem, we know how he died, surely the fact that I have identified him is enough?"

"You have to understand that the Australians are running the show here, they have a forensic team in place."

"I say again, nobody is doing a full post mortem on my brother. I have the dental records and that should be enough and secondly, why do we not have our own team here? Why are we relying on the Australians who aren't even at the morgue?"

"I think you misunderstood me. They aren't running it all. They are the country who have lost the most. They have sent a team out here and they are working with the Indonesians on the investigation. Until they are ready to do a post mortem, we will have to wait. We will then decide what the procedure is. They are currently analysing the bomb site."

After further questions Tobias is fuming: this man doesn't seem to know what the system is or who is running it, let alone what the next step is. Jon's is the first body to be identified and nobody seems to know what the procedure is.

Peter, our expat, suggests getting back in touch with David Magson. David advises Tobias to return to the morgue to see if they can find the Indonesian doctor who could verify the body with the dental records.

I am still without a plane ticket for the UK, so Tobias wants me to return to the hotel with Mike and sort out travel plans while he goes back to the morgue.

There Tobias is welcomed again by David Magson and Calvin. Both are businessmen in Bali who offered themselves as volunteers to the Honorary Consul at the Cat and Fiddle the day after the explosion. It seems almost the entire expat community have stepped forward to help. At a meeting the volunteers were allocated roles to assist the bereaved families as they arrived in Bali.

David manages to pin down one of the Australian forensic doctors who is unsure of the procedure. He advises Tobias to fill out an 'Australian Incident Form'. It then turns out that this is not the correct form and another one is produced. Finally, thanks to David speaking the local language, a translated Indonesian form is photocopied and Tobias sits down to fill out this 12-page document. It requires seven officials from Britain, Australia and Bali to help complete the form, so complicated are the questions. Codes, street names, hospital reference numbers, doctors names are all needed to ensure that the form will clear the various authorities and be released. It takes an hour to complete and Tobias insists that it is photocopied and distributed to all the country representatives so no one else will have the same problems.

The BBC crew have now latched on to these complications and Clive Myrie has managed to slip in with his camera crew. David Magson is not keen and says "Not now Rageh!". "I'm not Rageh (another BBC News Reporter). I'm Clive Myrie" comes the quick retort.

As the form is checked with the Indonesians, Tobias films his first interview. He walks down the *cul de sac* in front of the morgue with Clive and shares his horror at the bureaucracy and lack of British official assistance.

"There should be an official British team here helping us. An emergency response team. Maybe as many as 30 British people have died here, and as many are injured. How many deaths are needed before the British respond properly?"

His remarks are not aimed at Mark Wilson, the Honorary Consul, or the support provided by the ex-pat community, but at the Embassy in Jakarta and the Ambassador who came up for a day but returned back to Jakarta the Monday after the bombing.

Eventually an Indonesian doctor arrives and accepts the form. Once more Tobias observes the body bag being removed from the refrigerated container, opened, and the carrying out of the 'primary examination'(dental inspection). By the time the inspection is complete and the form signed and stamped it is past 5pm. Another hurdle has been jumped. So what next?

"We can't release the body until the Undertaker is here. We will have to wait until the morning" the doctor says. So we arrange a meeting with the repatriation company, who cover nearly all international school teachers, to meet us at the Cat and Fiddle next day. Finally they leave the morgue.

Mike and I return to the travel agent. Patiently he tries to arrange flights for us again. Having met Tobias and seen him in action Mike now decides to book his own flight home. "Now that Tobias is here, I can see that you are in good hands. I think it's time I went back home to Hong Kong." Of course he had his own grieving to do, for he was a good friend of Shane's. My guardian angel has completed his task.

Tobias and Pete return from the morgue and join us on the wicker chairs on our patio. I am somewhat elated. At least they have accomplished something, although Tobias is still flabbergasted that he has had to do it all himself. Poor Pete has hardly been home for the last four days and takes his leave. So we make our way back to the restaurant for some pizza. Although food is necessary, appetite is lacking.

It is now 8pm and a girl arrives in the middle of the meal to collect a photo of Jon. Clive's team from the BBC are putting together their broadcast and want a picture. Tobias offers to pick the photo up later. I am not keen, I really don't want to go walking about Kuta at night but Tobias insists. I am not going to leave him again. So we say goodnight to Mike and walk around the block to the Hard Rock Café.

It all seems so surreal, passing through the corridors of rooms to the BBC's press room. Their bedroom has been turned into a makeshift studio with TV gear sprawled everywhere. Clive shakes hands and returns the passport. "Would you like to see the clip we have done?"

We watch the editor rewind the clip and there is Tobias walking down the road behind the morgue, like a tourist guide showing someone round: "and over there is the lorry with my brother in it" he is saying. "Where's our man in a Panama hat? We feel very let down" then it cuts to Clive who has also interviewed Mark Wilson. "...He may not have a Panama hat but this is the man trying to deal with the British situation..."

"It should make the six o'clock news." We thank him and we make our way downstairs.

"You know Mum is probably going to see this, don't you?" I remark to Tobias.

"Do you think it will upset her?".

"Well, it will if she's taken by surprise. Jon's picture, in full size. On the six o'clock news."

"I think Mum would be very proud, it doesn't say anything negative, it's just saying how let down we feel." This is beginning to be the phrase of the day. "Maybe we should ring Janet (Mum's best friend and local vicar) and ask her to go round and sit with her."

Janet is a larger than life character who has been a friend of the family for the last 30 years and has watched Jon grow up. However Janet does not answer. It is Mickey, her husband. He explains that Janet isn't in but offers to sit with Mum instead. Tobias is right though. Although shaken she is very proud, both of Jon and Tobias.

It is now 11pm and we are very tired. We take a taxi back to our hotel and Tobias shows the first signs of stress by complaining to the taxi driver that he is deliberately taking us around in circles. The taxi driver has indeed taken us a long route, but this is because the main road, which once took you past the Sari Club and Paddy's Bar, is now closed.

17th October

The British now know that Tobias feels 'let down'. Bali is eight hours ahead of Britain. The Bali contingent is, through necessity, struggling with this crisis around the clock meanwhile Britain is asleep and playing catch-up eight hours later.

We have breakfast by the hotel pool and listen to the incessant Bali music in the background. "It's like elevator music gone wrong" Tobias muses. He is in better spirits after a night's sleep although he has been up since 5am, taking in the sunrise. Mike joins us, but the breakfast area is otherwise deserted, as are the streets outside the hotel empty of tourists, leaving desperate businesses to suffer the after-effects of a futile bomb.

Mike is due to fly off in the afternoon but he continues his vigil of support and we make our way to the Cat and Fiddle with quiet Pete. He apologises for Enrica's absence; she has had to stay at home with her children. Without realising it, we had developed into a team and we had a mission. If one of the team members is away their absence is felt by us all. Everyone, however, feels quite positive. A bit more paperwork and we will be on our way.

The Cat and Fiddle seems to have moved up a gear. A volunteer now stands guard by the entrance and all visitors are obliged to sign in and out. Tributes and flowers have started to arrive and are placed along the pavement. The pub is now closed to normal business and seems to be running as a mini crisis centre. A television has been set up, tuned into the BBC. Things certainly have improved.

Next to the drive is a small temple. Pete explains that there are many around, part of the religious observance being to make offerings – food, flowers, anything – to appease the Gods. Well, they will need a lot of appeasing this week.

The four of us sign in and are greeted by an official young woman. "Hello, I'm from the Consulate in Jakarta. How can I help you?"

Tobias moves straight in:"We were here yesterday, we are the Ellwoods."

However it is clear she doesn't have a clue who the Ellwoods are. "So, have you come to find a relative or friend?"

Tobias patiently explains that we are already at the next stage. Things clearly have a little way to go. "We were here yesterday. We have been through all this, I have already identified Jon Ellwood, my brother."

"Oh... what is the name again?"

"Can we speak to someone who was here yesterday?" Tobias asks, looking around for a familiar face. Lee from the Jakarta embassy, even Mrs Fluffy, somebody to keep the ball rolling. It is like a new shift has started and we are back to square one. Calvin sees us and says: "I'll tell them you are here". Mark Wilson approaches (well I thought it was Mark but it turns out to be his brother) introduces himself and says they will be with us in a minute.

Tobias starts muttering. "I can't believe this. You would have thought they would have a white board somewhere, saying who they have dealt with and at what stage they are. It's just common sense."

We order some drinks and wait for the next official. A middle-aged chap with a moustache introduces himself to us. He is Stephen Evans, the new Vice-Consul from Singapore. He is also an ex-police officer and immediately grasps the need to understand and communicate a process to the victim's families. He spends the rest of the day following us around and making copious notes. We are pioneering a path through this complex jungle of red tape. He wants to ensure other families can follow.

As we are waiting, Sue Speak, a jolly Scottish lady and a volunteer, goes past us with what seems to be the only flag she can find. "I'm off to the morgue to stake our place," she cries, as she waves the Union Jack, the small kind you would find on someone's desk. We smile.

It is now time for our meeting with the repatriation organisation, SOS International. They will take responsibility for flying the coffin back to the UK. Funny how you expect someone tall, large and assertive to walk in but then a petite, plainly dressed Balinese lady walks up and introduces herself as the woman from SOS.

Before we have a chance to do the introductions this little mouse shrieks "Calvin" and goes bright red. As does Calvin who is sitting with us "Oh hello, how are you ?" he says in his best David Niven voice.

"How are you?" she squeals.

It appears she was one of his long-lost girl-friends from many years ago. It is also apparent that it didn't end on a good note, for Calvin makes a fast exit, but not before whispering "Don't worry, she will take good care of you."

The SOS lady soon composes herself and gets down to business. She rings the undertaker on her mobile and arranges to meet him at the morgue. My fear of the morgue has subsided by now; in fact it feels right to be there. After all, that is where Jon is. This time we park down the side road from the morgue and walk straight up to the official entrance, now with plenty of guards.

Round the back of the lorries we find Sue Speak at her desk with another Scottish lady, Karen, manning the post. Sue has shut her local business to volunteer and Karen had sent both her children out of the country but has stayed herself, to help. Another David has been manning the morgue post since Sunday. It is his refrigerated truck that is now holding the few known British. His mother is sending food by the hour from their delicatessen to all the volunteers, which includes amazing home-made cookies. David buzzes about all day, helping anyone and everyone.

Despite having a team of eight now, no one knows what to do next. Tobias looks around and happens upon a list on the wall which gives the procedure for discharging a body from the morgue, one in Bahasa, one in English "What about this?" he says. "This tells us what to do." Frustration is creeping in. He turns to Stephen: "Maybe you should get a copy of this."

Sitting amongst 200 coffins is rather strange, especially when you are sitting on what will actually become someone's coffin. They come in all kinds of shapes and sizes, some short, some long, some ornamental, many very obviously DIY. Tobias comes back steaming "I can't believe this, We have to do another inspection."

We all retreat to our chill out-area on the coffins next to the desk with the British flag.

Two hours later and the undertaker, Gus, arrives. He looks like an Indonesian version of the Fat Controller. As the only undertaker on the island, he is an indespensable man and walks with an air of importance. He seems to have a bit of influence at the morgue; after all, this is his line of business. He is moved by the whole scale of things, and the sheer magnitude of the operation and confusion means he can not pull any strings today. Another primary inspection is needed by the Indonesian team and, until this happens he can do nothing. Subdued, he sits in the morgue office and waits.

The morgue is a hive of activity, becoming slightly more organised each day. Inside teams of Indonesian and Australian forensics go through bodies. There are Indonesian helpers moving body bags to and fro, as identifications are completed. Ice is delivered every three hours and placed on the 200 body bags lying everywhere. A lorry appears delivering more appropriate footwear for the helpers, many of whom are only wearing open sandals. Half an hour later, all the staff and volunteers are parading in brand new green wellies.

Next to the British table is the Australian desk, although we don't actually see any Australian families as such. They are no doubt being kept at their Consulate until such time as the morgue is ready with a positive identification of some kind. However there are a number of officials including an RAAF Padre, Peter Harvey, who makes himself known to us straight away. A very large chap, he has a cuddly physique and makes you feel safe. He never pushes for details.

At about 1pm Mike takes his leave. I will never forget his care, concern and patience. It seems amazing. He was just there, quietly present, but that was everything in my time of need. Selfless people such as Mike give you faith in humanity.

At 3pm we are still sitting waiting. "It'll happen; it just takes time." I keep saying to Tobias. Somebody asks if my brother is here. "Yes, both of them." I reply "One in there – the office – one in there – the truck."

Sue, observes that we will need to start sorting out the coffins. She says this more to Karen, the other volunteer than to me. "Who is going to write their names on them?"

"I'll do it if you want" I offer, anything is better than sitting on a coffin all day. So she finds a big, thick, black pen and the list of names. I take the opportunity to go to Jon's truck and write his name next to his number, '157'.

I notice some heavy, Balinese carved, wooden coffins in the corner of the barn. They are superior. Very ethnic. "Can we use one of these?" I ask "I don't see why not" replies Sue. So I select the top one. It is massive. I write Jon's name on the end 'Jon Ellwood 157. Rest in peace love from Mum, Dad, Tobias & Totty.'

'I feel OK now
I hugged him yesterday
And said goodbye
I felt the coldness of his body
He is dead and gone
Up there, somewhere
Somewhere in the stars
Where I can see him
And he can see me
This is just a body now
That we have to take home and put to rest.'

At 4pm I am still sitting on a coffin. Tobias observes yet another inspection. It almost doesn't happen, as they have lost Jon's file and with it his dental records. Fortunately Tobias has another photocopy in his rucksack. "This is why you need a proper emergency response team" he keeps saying to anyone who will listen "so these sorts of things don't happen". To add to the complications, the powers that be apparently change the format of the death certificate, so they are now looking for the new kind of certificate. Tobias can't believe it. After every hurdle there is yet another. He takes a breather and walks up to where I have chosen the coffin and for the first time he sees what I had written on it. The shock takes hold, it was so real there in writing; he simply bursts into tears.

After that, every time we want to talk we go and stand next to the coffin. It is as if it was part of Jon already. Tobias holds the side, leaning on it as he discusses the next proceedings with me. I tell him to keep calm. "I know, I know" he replies.

"No, I mean it, Tobias, these people will do anything to help you, but they can't cope with you getting impatient. Keep smiling and showing appreciation" and off he goes back into the quagmire.

Tobias returns with Jon's wallet. "Are you ready for this?" he asks. He has stumbled across the Belongings Department which is struggling to determine its own procedure for release of personal effects. Tobias signs a chit and takes the bag of possessions before they design a new procedure.

We wander over to Jonathan's coffin. Tobias opens the plastic bag from which a black, singed, half-burnt wallet tumbles out. Tobias opens it up. Hundreds of half burnt dollars and melted credit cards fall out. It smells as if it is still burning. The black ash flits around as the papers fall apart in his hands.

"What shall we do with it?" he asks.

"Throw it away" I say. "No… keep the cards, we may need them."

I don't really know why. It just seems strange to throw Jon's things away. It's just a material thing. It's not Jon. I am becoming numb to anything now. So Tobias puts it back in the plastic bag and in his rucksack.

Tobias is approached by Sky TV to do an interview. He makes it sound as if we are about to wrap the day up and walk out with Jon, so they wait all afternoon to get a shot of the coffin from behind the wall. I grumpily comment that, in my opinion, Sky television is the *Sun* of the TV world but nevertheless we speak to them. After all we had a point to make, that we feel 'let down'. Tobias talks about the need for a proper British crisis team. I take the opportunity to add my bit about teachers whose lives are dedicated to cultural understanding being killed. Sky are more interested in Tobias's problems which seem to be escalating as the afternoon goes on.

Gus the undertaker, who had disappeared into the office building – which now resembled a Chinese betting shop with papers and people being furiously exchanged – returns to say he can not take ownership of the body until it had been embalmed. It is an obvious requirement when transporting a body a long distance, but why has no one explained this to us earlier? Gus wants to get away, but Tobias insists he remain at our base by the coffins whilst he tries to find an embalmer.

As if by chance, an area behind the morgue building has been screened off to allow members of The Kenya Disaster Company embalming team to set up shop. Apparently that is their thing, embalming mass bodies in crises. They are efficient despite their appearance. They have baseball caps with Kenyan Disaster Team embroidered on with their logo. All have beards and all wear shorts and look like *ZZ Top* on holiday. They are here to do business, although so far not one of the 200 bodies have come their way. Tobias finds them playing cards. "I've got a body that needs embalming. Can you help? "Of course, if you have the paper work." Tobias produces every official document he has accumulated. The papers are in order, and we are in business.

Tobias remains to ensure there are no more hiccups. As he reiterated later "I now know more about embalming fluids than I care to know."

In the meantime, a nice American lady called Sue approaches with a gift of a rose. I ask who it is from and she replies 'the people of Bali'. Lee, the American from the Crisis Centre, arrives. He is a genuinely good guy.

He and his friend Sam (the key identifier), who also plonked himself exhaustedly down beside us, have been part of the aftermath since midnight on Saturday. They have been living in Bali for 16 years. Sam looks like a carpenter, wearing a tool belt full of helpful equipment. He sits cleaning his glasses with his t-shirt, slumped in exhaustion.

"Go home Sam, you've been here too long." Lee says.

"Yeah, yeah I will eventually."

I show them my picture of Jon, another attempt to turn him into a person. I show it to Scottish Sue, who presses it back into my hand and turns her face away to hide the tears. She is not ready to accept that these are real people. Sam however, seems pleased to see a real person. After all, he has seen enough burnt people in the last few days; he has seen Doomsday first hand.

Our time at the morgue, with the endless hours of waiting, allow faces to become familiar and conversations to develop. People are becoming aware of the progress we have made and the reality that the first body could soon be flying out. They are all willing us on. Sam and Lee seems to be just hovering to see at least one body be taken out of this God-awful place. And it is an awful place, the stench, the heat, the thought of lines of bodies lying sweltering in the sun, just waiting…

You are constantly aware of the horror you are part of. One French chap arrives to look for his friend. He opens 53 body bags before he comes out wailing in desperation and agony over what he had seen. He simply can't find his friend and it is all too much. Tobias says he would have opened every bag until he found Jonathan. But for some it would have been so futile: there are many that have perished into unidentifiable beings.

It's 5pm and I am still sitting on the coffin and there is still no sign of the body being released. Some staff try to persuade me that my chosen coffin for Jon is not ideal. Tobias explains that we have become attached to it and are keeping it. People keep remarking how well we are holding it together but it is only necessity and the adrenaline that keep things moving. The Sky News team bid their farewell, even they can't hold on forever.

Then Peter's mobile 'phone rings. It is GMTV (after all it is now morning in England). "No, Tobias" I press him "You can't talk to them, they sensationalise everything". In the event I am quite wrong, for it is thanks to the morning news such as GMTV and Sky that the Foreign Secretary, Jack Straw, actually hears about the bureaucratic nightmare we are facing. Journalists question him directly and ask what he is doing to help the Ellwood family. (I am sure his first thought was 'Who on earth is this Ellwood family?')

Pete is still with us and in Mike's absence we rely on his mobile to communicate with Mum and Dad. Enrica is also here and our SOS woman has also sat patiently all afternoon. Stephen from the Singapore Embassy must have moved on to a new note book, he is scribbling so much. All of us are waiting for the 'go' from the embalming team.

At last Tobias comes over to us accompanied by five Indonesian helpers and, to our delight, and under his constant instruction, the six lift the coffin I have selected and march back into the embalming area. Jon is placed inside and the lid of the coffin is fitted on top. Tobias now has another document to add to his pile, the embalming certificate. What next? Surely it is time for the undertaker.

Just when things seemed to be speeding up, again the portcullis comes crashing down. The undertaker has gone walkabout. Twenty minutes ago he told the SOS lady that "he would be back." She 'phones him, again and again. But no reply. We wait and wait. I start to stalk up and down like a caged animal. I can't believe it, what did he bloody think he was doing? The only undertaker on the whole island and he does a runner.

Two hours later still no show. I am fuming. This time it is Tobias's turn to calm me down. He decides to call it a day. In fact the whole morgue is shutting down. Teams have left and a guard is at the door of the morgue for the night (apparently a body went missing last night).

The SOS lady, very apologetic, promises to deliver Gus to us tomorrow morning at 9am. Apparently he has got 'confused.' Enrica explains later that this is a common Balinese trait. If things get too much they just leave, no comment, they just go until they don't feel pressurised again.

For goodness sake, bodies are this man's bread and butter; what is he doing getting confused? But then again maybe the enormity of it has hit him as it did the rest of us at different times. After all, this atrocity didn't just hit us foreigners. It has also destroyed the Bali paradise that was and killed Balinese people as well. Maybe he has his own reasons for leaving the morgue.

We arrange to regroup at 9am. Stephen 'the scribe', goes off to write-up his notes and Tobias and I go in to say goodbye to Jon. Walking through the bodies is almost familiar now. All those black and yellow bags seem to disappear into a haze.

Jon's coffin is now raised up on two planks on a large blue tarpaulin. I tape the rose onto the coffin lid. He is no longer a body in a bag, he is Jonathan Mark Ellwood, age 37 in a proper, dignified coffin.

It has been an eternity of a day. Pete drops us off at the hotel. We walk up to the reception and pick up our messages. Then, out of nowhere, a camera team jumps us. "Hi are you British?" asks the bloke. I raise my eyebrows and give Tobias a look that says "no more interviews".

"Er... yes" says Tobias.

Whoosh, the camera lights go on. The fuzzy microphone dangles above us and they are filming.

"We are from *London Tonight*. So, what do you think about Jack Straw saying all British citizens should get out of Bali asap?'

Tobias can see I'm not in the mood.

"Well, we aren't leaving until we can take our brother, who was killed in the bomb, with us."

The interviewer's face drops completely.

"Oh, my God, turn it off guys."

The cameraman lowers the camera and the journalist shows complete and utter remorse for what his job is forcing him to do.

"I'm so, so sorry, I would never have asked you so coldly. We were just looking for tourists in the area. Er... I totally understand if you don't want to carry on."

He is utterly contrite. Tobias forgives him instantly.

"No, it's alright." Whoosh, the camera goes back up "We've just had a very long day, dealing with bureaucracy and having little support to get my brother out."

I am ready to flop and once the camera has gone we walk into the hotel to find another reporter waiting for us. Matthew Campell has just flown in from Paris and is due to write a few pieces on the aftermath of the bomb. He recognises that we had had a long day and suggests supper.

"It's OK, the paper will pay." So we catch a taxi round to the Hard Rock. I must say I warm to him. I am very cagey about journalists. Mum has told me on the 'phone that some daily tabloid isn't taking no for an answer and are sitting in a car outside her house. One villager asked them politely to move on but it took a stronger version from our neighbour, Simon, to give them the message and even then they just went further down the road.

This journalist however is friendly and unassuming. We are hungry and appreciate the opportunity of a good meal. He jots down Tobias's and my comments as we eat. We talk about the trials of the last few days and our ordeal with Mrs Fluffy at the Cat and Fiddle. Tobias comes out with the line "We want movers and shakers, not huggers and hand holders."

The Hard Rock is thronged with journalists. The Sky team walks past and waves and another BBC journalist, Ben Brown, comes over and says hello. Matthew seems to know him from another stint and they chat briefly. Tobias takes the opportunity to whisper a few words to me.

"Be careful what you say Totty" apparently I am starting to rabbit on. "You don't want to start talking about how you are a tree-hugger; they will quote anything and twist it." And it is true, I am ready to tell this guy anything, he is so nice and understanding. I am just trying to point out what a peaceful person I am but Tobias is right.

The resulting article is nothing for us to worry about; indeed we appreciated his efforts to spell out our plight in detail. We are both proud to be British and complaining about our own government does not seem right. But the British in Bali need help and it is thanks to people like Clive Myrie and Matthew Campell that they eventually get it.

We part at the taxi rank and Tobias persuades me to walk home via the beach. So we make our way in the dead of the night, recapping the long, long day. The beach is very dark as the town's lights fade away. Tobias hands me his wallet and says "hold these".

"Why?" I asked innocently.

"In case anyone jumps us, you ninny."

Well, I wasn't scared before but I am terrified now. It is very spooky and everywhere are those graveyard circles of sticks in the ground with ashes inside. We return to the hotel without incident only to discover that the Melasti Beach Bungalows doesn't actually have an entry onto the beach.

We are forced to climb the eight foot high wall that is visible from our balcony.

We flop into the wicker chairs and once again I need to 'phone the rounds; Matthew, Mum and Dad. It must be just as traumatic at their end, sitting by the 'phone, not knowing what is happening, watching news bulletins and waiting for information, the Foreign Office and calls from me.

We must have done some good though. For the Foreign Office are taking note that the Ellwood family 'feel let down' and Baroness Amos, a Foreign Office minister, is now on her way to Bali to find out what is going on. Tobias knows of her: "She's a mover and a shaker, Totty, if anybody can get things done, she will."

18th October

Tobias is still struggling with jet-lag. At 5am he gets up, leaves the hotel and walks down the road to he bomb site. By 6 o'clock I am awake too. Tobias comes back with a mission.

"Let's go round and have another look, Totty."

"I have no desire to go there whatsoever."

"Come on, Totty, you'll really regret it if you don't. It's the last place Jon was."

So, as the sun rises, we wander the silent streets of Kuta. Little roads lead into more little roads, all containing closed shops. The place is desolate. As we walk we wonder if Jon and Shane took this route. They must have walked along the road, with no idea that around the corner everything would end.

Jalan Legian, the main road, is now blocked off to traffic, so we are able to walk down the middle. It was obviously the happening place, plenty of bars and souvenir shops on either side. As we approach we see hundreds upon hundreds of floral tributes that have been placed along both sides of the road. Large white sheets are hanging stretched out between tall posts, all covered with writing: commiserations, condolences and heartfelt comments.

At least 100 metres of tragic tapestry provide visitors with an opportunity to vent their grief. The floral tributes are massive and impressive, with printed writing in the centre saying things like 'The Balinese Police send condolences to the families of the victims of the Bali Bomb' 'The Intercontinental Hotel wishes to express their utmost sympathy for the victims of the Bali Bomb' all lined up along the path to where the Sari Club once stood. As we get closer, more and more windows are cracked and broken, smashed by the impact of the blast.

We pass Paddy's Bar on the right. It is now a shell, with remnants of the bar, tables and chairs where people had stood and chatted, now just a black carcass. Broken glass is everywhere. To the left is a vast area where the Sari Club would have been. Once a place of life and laughter, it is now a twisted wreck of metal concrete and rubble and memories.

The actual area is sectioned. A group of Balinese singers chant prayers, as they have every morning since the bomb. A scattering of people stand around, taking in the contrast of the peaceful singing with the horror of the crater. We return to the hotel for breakfast, the only guests at 8am. There are 12 staff on duty in the restaurant.

For the third day in a row we head off for the morgue, hoping Gus will be back on form. Fortunately he is just arriving with the SOS lady and she is not going to let him out of her sight again. We settle into our usual positions, me at the British desk and Tobias in the morgue with the undertaker.

It seems that Britain is taking things more seriously now. The British Ambassador from Jakarta has arrived again in Bali and intends to grace us with his presence. I resist asking him why he deserted the British cause and returned to Jakarta on Monday morning. Stephen 'the scribe', the Singapore Vice-consul, is there with his notepad and another police officer from Scotland Yard is hovering around. More over-dressed British staff are rolling in, looking very pink as they adjust to the heat. Tobias takes the opportunity of reiterating his idea about an emergency response team and the need for a process of procedure. It is quite apparent these people are arriving because the TV reports are true. Britain has been slow to react, but now Baroness Amos has landed and the Ambassador has to dash. He has a VIP to meet.

Undertaker Gus's job is not a big one and usually he would take the casket away to be cremated, as is normal in Bali. On this occasion he seems rather out of his depth and does not know how to secure the lid of this enormous coffin. Tobias, David, Gus, Stephen, Enrica and some Indonesian helpers stand around the coffin pondering the problem.

The type of coffin that I have chosen has an extremely thick lid. A hammer and nail simply will not do. What follows is like a scavenger hunt: Pete and David both go to find screws and a drill. Pete arrives back first. An Indonesian proceeds to drill in the screws but they keep breaking. Tobias takes over. He can't believe it: here he is drilling the screws into his brother's coffin. Ironic really, the drill is the one item Jon and Tobias were always borrowing from each other. "Has anyone seen my drill?" Jon would say "I bet that Tobias has got it." They bickered incessantly accusing each other of borrowing tools without permission.

Somehow the screws just won't drill in properly and Tobias ends up hammering the last bits in. "They are going to struggle to open that at the Coroner's Inquest" Tobias says triumphantly.

The undertaker then announces that sealing wax is needed to be dripped onto the screw heads before he can write up a sealing certificate. We do not even ask why he failed to mention this earlier. Pete is duly dispatched again to purchase some sealing wax.

Finally our undertaker is happy and the Scotland Yard officer can stick his official Customs and Excise label on it to say he has witnessed it. "With any luck that should hinder them from actually opening it at the other end."

It really does seem as if we are nearing the end of our stay at the morgue. Everyone leaves the area and Tobias and I prepare to say our farewell to Jon. We take the Australian padre Peter Harvey and his padre colleague in with us. His colleague is quite humorous. At one point he is given the drill to hold. "Are you going to put that down" asks Harvey before we start the prayers. He looks around, there wasn't anywhere appropriate to put it. "Someone might trip over it." So he holds the drill while Harvey reads a section from the Bible about going onward on one's journey. It is quite apt considering (as was the drill). Tobias and I say goodbye again and tell Jon we will see him in Aldbury.

Eight small but strong Indonesians carry the huge coffin marked 157 through the corridors containing black and yellow body bags, stepping carefully over each one, to the ambulance now waiting by the gates. All the heads turn and smile at us, pleased that our ordeal is finally over and one body is at last returning home.

Peter Barnett, a helper at the Cat and Fiddle, who had been manning the 'phones and dealing with administration, has sorted out our tickets. Jon will be taken straight to the airport where he will go on the same plane as us to Singapore.

Good news has come from Mum and her liaison officers that the Government will be paying for the flights of the bereaved families, (although at the same time discouraging anyone to go). "I should think so too," I said to Enrica "I hope it's business class as well, I've never flown business class and if there is one time in my life when I think I deserve it, then this is it."

Watching Jon go off in the ambulance I am less euphoric than I had expected. Part of me doesn't want to allow the coffin out of my sight; it has become part of my life and is my only current connection to him. We are of course pleased, but the next phase is also forbidding as it will involve grieving. No more adrenalin pumping through your veins as you rush from obstacle to obstacle but coping instead, like normal mourners, with the excruciating loss of a loved one.

Pete's 'phone rings. Baroness Amos is hoping to meet us at her hotel where a reception is taking place. Tobias and I discuss this. "I am not going to some fancy reception to meet some Baroness" I argue vehemently. "If she wants to see us, tell her to come to us." Tobias agrees, although not so vehemently.

"Could you pass the message on that we are going back to the Cat and Fiddle, we feel comfortable there and that's where we want to spend the next few hours before we go to the airport. We have people to thank and see before we go and that is very important to us."

Pete supports our idea and is happy to pass on our message. We say our goodbyes to so many people at the morgue. Many who have watched us over the days burst into tears as we hug them goodbye.

We collect our luggage en route to the Cat and Fiddle and, on arrival, flop into seats in the shade. This is the first time since arriving when we both have nothing to do. It was an odd feeling. We order a plate of fish and chips each.

The Cat and Fiddle has a welcoming atmosphere, people eating and sitting around, whilst at the back the Consulate team bustle about. For the first time I look at the décor, the theme of the nursery rhyme on the walls. Another photocopier has arrived and there is an air of organisation about the place. Stephen takes Tobias to one side and thanks him for his help. David Magson comes over and apologises for not being with us today. After four days at the morgue, it has all become too much for him and he needs a rest. He is delighted to hear we were on our way home.

A message has come through from the Jakarta Embassy implying that the help of people like David, although well intended, is not always of the most benefit. They should steer clear of certain areas such as the morgue and not discuss personal issues with the victim's families. This is astonishing because it is the volunteers who have helped us through the ordeal, people like David, Pete, Enrica, Calvin, not to mention Sam, who had rummaged through nearly 200 bodies to find some sort of identification. They are the heroes of the tragedy; maybe they didn't save someone's life but they are the support network that stood up to the crisis and served from the heart. The volunteers were, in effect, filling the gap for the Emergency Response Team that Tobias speaks about.

Lee from the Hong Kong Consulate reappears to say that Baroness Amos is still keen to meet us. She has now changed her plans to come straight to the Cat and Fiddle. Let the Mountain come to Mohammed. I am secretly quite pleased, for it shows that our cause does matter to her.

Soon Indonesian police start arriving in numbers, followed by a posse of officials speaking into their shirt cuffs and scouting the area out. More men in suits turn up and finally a huge convoy arrives. Baroness Amos enters the Cat and Fiddle surrounded by Indonesian officials, Foreign Office bag carriers and the media.

I have never met Baroness Amos. My only experience of a Parliamentary VIP was Tom King (Lord King of Bridgwater) when he was an MP and Tobias's previous employer. I imagined her to be an old lady with the bouffant hair of the Conservative blue rinse brigade. However Tobias tells me that she is a 'Blair babe' and an efficient one at that. So I am pleasantly surprised when she steps regally out of her car. She is like an African gazelle, long black linen dress with a white shawl down one side and a presence about her that is certainly not blue-rinse.

Her young assistant sits down opposite me, to the left of Tobias, and takes notes, sweltering in the heat in her long black sleeves. I sit between the Baroness and Tobias. Baroness Amos is indeed deeply sorry and concerned about our ordeal and listens very carefully to everything we have to say. Tobias puts forward his ideas about a proper emergency response team and she says that it had been brought up before but never put in place. We must have talked for about 15 minutes and then she has to move on to Mark Wilson. We both feel she was genuinely sorry. Not only that, but that she will act on what had been said. After all, if something good can come out of our ordeal then at least we have not let Jon down.

****

FOREIGN AND COMMONWEALTH OFFICE PRESS RELEASE FRIDAY 18 OCTOBER 2002

Jack Straw said today:

'I said yesterday that we would look into the Ellwood family's complaint about the support they received in Bali. Baroness Amos is in Bali, and has spoken to the families of all those who have died or are missing. While they all said that they appreciated the support we had given, it is clear that the Ellwood family did not receive the standard of service they were entitled to expect. Baroness Amos has apologised to the Ellwoods and I

repeat that apology. Given the deep distress the family were already suf-
fering, I am sorry that we added to their burden. I have offered to see the
family on their return to the UK'

****

Tobias is still doing the rounds talking to people so I take the opportunity to ring Mum to keep her up to par. She now has the go-ahead to organise the funeral, which will be a week on Saturday.

We take our leave from Mark Wilson. "I hope you don't feel I was per-
sonally attacking you, Mark" Tobias tells him. Mark smiled, looking
very tired and worn out. Tobias adds: "We really appreciate everything
you have done for us and realise how stretched you are. We just hope
things will be easier for the next family."

Mark has a lovely, soft northern accent that makes you think of Wallace
and Grommit. "Well, so do I. You have done us a big favour. Thank you.
I'll have to get myself a Panama hat now" and he laughs.

We bid our farewells to Enrica and the rest of the team and make our way
to the airport with Pete. Clive Myrie is waiting for us there; the first
British family to take home their loved one. They film us going through
to the departure hall. Unfortunately I crash straight into a pillar with my
trolley, but I don't think they use that bit of footage. It was comforting to
know we were leaving on the same plane as Jon.

To our delight Singapore Airlines has up-graded us to business class. I am
chuffed. I know how pleased Jon would be. He had reached a point in his
life where he was earning enough to fly long-haul business class. "Once
you fly business, you never want to go back to riff-raff" he used to say.

Going Home

Jon flies direct to London and is sent to a Coroner's Court in Fulham, and remains there until the Inquest. We have a stop-over in Singapore where we spend the night in the Orchard Hotel, a favourite with pilots and crew. They are also holding the South-East Asia anti-terrorism Conference. Needless to say we don't bother to attend. After some more waiting in the business lounge the next day, we start the final leg of our long journey home. Singapore Airlines are fantastic, although it does get rather tiring hearing "We are sorry for your loss". It is a catch 22 situation though and continues for many weeks: if someone doesn't say anything you resent it, and if they do you have to vary your answer.

"We are sorry for your loss."

Face drops. "Thank you." I hate it, somehow it is like someone rubbing it in

"I'm so sorry".

"Yes, well, so am I." Others wouldn't know what to say.

"My condolences for your family."

And others would gush all over you.

"I am so, so sorry."

"Yes, well, it's happened" I develop a whole range of responses. None seem to be appropriate and when you are feeling so numb you don't want anything to nudge open the door of grief. You hold it together and fob people off. "Yes, it's a tragedy."

On the other hand if anyone so much as ignores the issue you seethe inside. How dare they not consider your grief, your brother and the disaster that has struck. Then again some people make the oddest remarks as they too don't know what to say. "It's very final" one friend commented. Well, yes, death normally is.

We arrive at Heathrow where a little, efficient-looking lady with a walkie-talkie appears on the plane and asks us to wait while everyone disembarks. Tobias is quite put out. Surely we should be getting off first? Apparently, they were waiting for the 'go' from the police. We don't realise that at the gate our next entourage is waiting; two police-officers, Mum and Janet and Tobias's girl-friend Hannah.

Poor Mum. So pleased to see us, so proud and so forlorn. Her face sunk with sadness, her hug full of grief. We are the only two left and she knows it as she holds us so tightly. We sit on a little buggy and are driven to the police office. She holds my hand all the way.

Kevin and Jerome, our policemen, have been assigned to us through Hertfordshire Constabulary. They are now our new team and have been liaising with Mother since Monday. Wearing official tags we are taken through some winding back ways at Heathrow where, treated like VIPs, we evade queues and lurking press and they even drive us home.

Home is Aldbury where I grew up with Jon and Tobias. Even when as a family we moved to Vienna, Aldbury was the little village we always returned to. Both brothers had attended the village school and it has been our family home for over 30 years. It is where our roots are, the global family returning for Christmas, Easter and summer to congregate, retreat, regroup and then venture back into the world.

Walking into my parents' house is like walking into a time-warp: it hasn't changed in my life-time and is full of Jon memories. Jon on the sofa, Jon standing in the kitchen with his arms folded. Jon in the morning, making a cup of coffee before his bath, the noises from that very same bath of his wallowing in the water like a hippo. Jon at my wedding, Jonathan rolling in once the pub shut for a philosophical chat at midnight.

It is now late at night and we are all sitting in the kitchen having our cups of tea. The table is piled full of letters from Jon's colleagues, friends, his students and villagers. There are even letters from complete strangers, who have seen Jon's picture on the television or read Mother's article in *The Independent* (Appendix One). Many letters I can't bear to read. You start a line and the tears begin. Best put it aside until later.

Kevin is a tall, friendly officer who soon has Tobias sussed. The first thing he says is: "Just to explain our role here. We are Family Liaison Officers assigned to you by the Hertfordshire police force. We are here to help you, provide you with information and answer any questions you may have." He adds smiling, "But to quote Tobias, we're not Mrs Fluffy." Everyone laughs and Tobias sighs with relief.

Jerome is equally friendly. They balance each other out well. My experience of the police is limited. Our local bobby, PC Fisher used to cycle between the villages. The worst problems our village currently seems to have is too many ducks on the pond and if there should be a cull or not.

Finally our two police liaison officers depart. Janet walks home and Hannah and Tobias retire to their room. It is just Mum and me in the kitchen. I can't bear it. Once again I am stifled by this enormous grief. I force myself to read a letter.

****

To Mr Ellwood

I keep expecting you to walk into History class, it is so hard. I see you sitting in your chair with your legs crossed, a pencil behind your ear, with your nose in a history book. I miss our gossiping before history class started. We had fun while we learnt. I knew that whenever I needed help I could walk into your office, where you would close your laptop, and you would spend however long it took to go through my work until I understood. I hope you know how much I appreciated your hard work and patience. I took it for granted that every one of my teachers would be there to see me graduate, but you will be there in my heart.

You helped me through my move from Wales to Vietnam by talking to me, I am truly grateful. I know that if you could see me writing this you would laugh at me drawing lines to make sure my sentences are straight – you always teased me that I was so organised. I miss the way you nodded your head when you were concentrating on what someone was telling you. But most of all I miss seeing your sunburnt face – complete with white sunglass lines around your eyes!

Forever in my thoughts

Victoria Harris (Year 12 pupil at HCM, Vietnam)

****

You can choke back emotional pain only so much. It is sitting there waiting for an opportunity. If you are clever you find distractions, every day, automatic functions and then you aren't forced to feel. I don't want to feel this pressing heaviness, it is too large, too incomprehensible. How can a bomb have changed our lives? It is as if I have been watching Totty in Bali for a week, in a foreign place, going through the motions of a film. Now, in the warmth of our kitchen in Aldbury, where I can see Jon leaning against the cupboard, with his arms folded avoiding argument by saying "I'm sure it is" his absence is even harder to bear.

I sit in the rocking chair while Mum, still in her coat, strokes my hands saying "My, poor little girl, my poor Totty" and the tears roll out. Still I'm not ready. I can't face it. Pull yourself together Totty, don't cry, if you cry you won't ever stop. "No, poor Jonathan, why our Jonathan?" still the tears roll down but I can't feel anything except the pressing against my heart.

The next few days roll by. People ring up, people visit, flowers arrive. Kevin and Jerome pop in to discuss the funeral and the pending Australian Memorial Service, but more importantly the Inquest has taken place and Jonathan has been taken to Metcalfe's Funeral Services in Berkhamstead.

My father arrives from Vienna and we arrange to go and see the coffin. It is odd, going to see the coffin. To me it represents Bali. If I had my way I would never bury Jonathan and just put the coffin somewhere so I can see it. It is so beautiful and holds the spirit of Bali in its carvings. Mum thinks that is unusually morbid, but then my morgue experience had been morbidly unusual.

When someone old dies, you expect it. It is a normal and natural. The Sari Club and Paddy's Bar were thronging with relatively young people, meeting up for a drink, a dance, a chat, a post rugby get-together, with expectations and dreams of a long and bright future. Couples, singles, families all with aspirations for the next day, the next week, the next year. So when so many, so young die unexpectedly, the reaction is initially shock and then an aching for the wasted life.

Dad and I enter Metcalfe's Chapel of Rest. My initial reaction is, how on earth do they get the coffin round the corners of these tiny, tight corridors? Still in functional, morgue-mode I feel I am doing a very practical thing showing Dad the way to Jonathan. The coffin has been laid in the appropriately named Aldbury Room. Lots of pictures of Aldbury hang on the walls. I wonder, rather perversely, who is supposed to be looking at them, and do they have a set for each place in the area, according to where the dead person has lived?

We find Jonathan's coffin at waist height on a collapsible trolley. The Bali rose is still taped firmly on the top (actually I had been quite persistent and attempted to staple-gun it down). I stroke the wood, as does Dad. It is smooth and thick and it feels comfortable for me to see again, affirming that we have managed to get him home. After a while I go out and leave Dad alone. I am already at the next step, further on than him. I said my goodbyes in Bali. After all, this is just his coffin and his body, his spirit to my mind, is in Bali.

"Let's go to London" says Matt

"Why would I want to go London?" I ask.

"It'll do you good, get you out of here, away from all of this."

I am too tired to argue. It is the middle of the night and we are strangers, separated by two weeks and a life-time. Matt has left the children with his mother, who has flown to Penang, in order to allow him to return back to England for the funeral. He is on Penang time and I am still on Bali time.

Once again I get up at 4am and meet Tobias in the kitchen. We scoff our cereal and sit and ponder, only to depart to our respective bedrooms and try and get some more sleep. So when I wake up for the second time it is almost a surprise to see Matt lying next to me. He repeats his idea. "We'll catch the train up, go to a gallery, see if Kathy wants to meet us for lunch" So I agree. I have spent nearly two weeks being Totty Ellwood, sister of Jon Ellwood, who is now dead in a coffin. Here is an opportunity to remember the other side of my life.

We go up on the train. Kathy, an old friend, is delighted at the prospect of seeing us and arranges to meet us in Covent Garden. It is surreal, all the people pursuing their own lives, all with independent little missions. People on the train, reading their papers, answering their mobiles, staring out of the window, then the hustle and bustle of Euston station and more people on the tube. Standing, sitting, silent, chatting, staring, ignoring others as the train bumps along. Everyone is being so normal. I want to stand up and shout: MY BROTHER WAS IN THE BALI BOMB, but no-one bats an eye-lid even though I am screaming it in my head.

Why don't they know? Can't they not tell by just looking at me? The last time I had felt this was after giving birth. Two weeks after having Felicity my mother persuaded Matt and me that Felicity would be fine with her for an hour. I should go out. So we went to the pub and again no-one seemed to notice that I was a different person; a mother.

Now I am walking around London with this earth shattering knowledge about myself and it is inside of me, no-one can see it. How can something so phenomenal be so invisible? The world does stop for you, there isn't any sense in anything; you function, you talk, you breathe but these are all automatic, your world ceases to turn, at least for the time being.

It is nice to see Kathy and it is good to re-bond with Matt. By the afternoon we are holding hands and he is my knight in shining armour, flown in to look after me. But by 2pm I have had enough. I want to go back to Aldbury. I can't stand the isolation of my pain. I want to return to the house where grief is an open book.

Other cultures seem to have mourning sussed. The Chinese lock themselves into their house for a week. They don't come out at all. Apparently this does cause numerous arguments but at least they are given an opportunity to get it out of their system. The Indians announce it to the world by shearing the hair of the eldest son in the family. So everyone knows. There are no questions, no embarrassments, no explanations necessary.

Although our whole village knows, indeed it seems the whole world knows, (Jon has been on the front of most of the national newspapers), some people talk as if nothing has happened. Others, who knew Jon well, come round and sit on the sofa and cry. You, the bereaved, are then mopping them up. Some will come round and just sit... and then leave.

Flowers are delivered two or three times a day. The corridors are overflowing. The 'phone rings; some friend of Mother's, Tobias's, Jon's or mine. Sometimes we just want to ignore the 'phone, but then Mum answers it. One is a very close friend of Mum's who has just opened the *Weekly Telegraph* in South Africa to see Jon's picture plastered on it. She has known Jon since he was four.

More letters come pouring in. By now Tobias has developed a keen filing system, placing letters in plastic folders marked Pendley Shakespeare Festival, Ho Chi Minh, Past schools, Village, Dad, Tobias, Mum, Totty. E-mails are printed out and added for when Mother replies with thanks.

The funeral has to be organised and hymns chosen. I don't normally believe in fate but this is a coincidence: The book falls open on *For the healing of the nations*, a hymn pleading for peace and conciliation. My choice is made.

By the time we return from London, it is late afternoon and Kevin and Jerome are due to discuss the funeral. Tobias is absent. "He must be still at the church doing his interview with *Newsnight*", Mum tells me. I can't believe it; he has gone solo! He tells me afterwards that he would have done it with me but I was in London; clearly my days with the press are on their way out. So be it, I haven't taken to it anyway, whereas Tobias is getting more eloquent as time goes on. Our friend Hugh Wilson was rehearsing his solo for the funeral in the church, so they manage to get some footage of that, which results in a very nice piece.

Kevin and Jerome arrive and once more we all huddled round the kitchen table. "The thing is we don't know how much press interest there will be, but we need to make arrangements for them. It is the first British funeral: it's bound to arouse some interest."

Tobias has realised this. "We've already discussed this with Huw Bellis, the Vicar. We don't want cameras in or around the church. We have said our bit and the funeral is private."

"You will need to make a statement which is handed out to them then."

"OK I'll write something up."

Our next subject is the Australian Memorial Service. We arrange to drive up together, including my father. Once again it strikes me as rather sad that he isn't part of all these proceedings. He is staying elsewhere with his partner; decisions are being made without him. Divorce gets in the way of everything, even death.

The service isn't until 5pm and we drive up after lunch: Kevin, Jerome, Matthew, another police officer, Tobias, Dad and me. It takes place at Westminster Cathedral and has been organised by the Australian Consulate. The Queen, Prince Charles and Prince Philip attend along with politicians from all parties. Again it is rather surreal: stepping outside of the personal box of tragedy this is an opportunity to share the grief of and offer respect to the families of the other 203 people who died.

Russell Ward, a Hertfordshire fireman who happened to be on holiday in Bali at the time and who had helped carry people out of the burning night clubs has been asked to light the candle in memory of the victims. All the victims' families sit at the front. At the end of the service we are led down some steep steps into the crypt for coffee. This is an opportunity to speak to Foreign Office people and also for the families to talk to each other.

Of all the bereaved families there we are amongst the most fortunate, for Jon is home. Some families went out but were unable to return with a body. Some had wanted to go out but were advised not to travel. One couple have lost their daughter and niece, both 18-years-old and on their first big trip abroad. Nearly six weeks later, at a subsequent memorial service held in Bali, they were still struggling with the authorities.

We head back, sad and upset by the impact of so many bereft families. We are exhausted. It is the eve of the funeral and I still haven't written my Eulogy. While we are in London, Jon is brought to the Church in Aldbury welcomed by Mum, Janet and Vicar Huw with a short service. He really is home now, as Tobias and I had promised.

The Funeral

Jet-lag and anxiety make me wake up at 4am. I creep downstairs to the laptop and, in the darkness of the night, write my funeral speech. "I think of Jonathan…" the words flow and I know it will be alright. I print it out and go back to bed.

We arrange to meet Dad at the church at 10am to practice my speech. Bizarre as it may seem to have a funeral rehearsal, it gives us all an opportunity to feel the coffin, feel the emotions and feel Jonathan with us before the public join us. We walk around the coffin. Tobias can smell it too. It smells of morgue: that distinct smell is still there.

Mum has decorated the coffin with golden orchids sent by Jon's previous Head all the way from the Philippines. A huge wreath of beautiful yellow roses, from the school in Vietnam, is placed at the front and The European Council of International Schools' bright blue banner is laid across the stand, all symbolising his place in the international school family.

Tobias practises his speech. Hannah and Matthew sit at the back, while Dad and I occupy a pew. Mum walks around the coffin sketching the Bali carvings. Tobias climbs up to the podium and starts: "The Cat in the Hat" he jokes.

We stop smiling once he starts Shakespeare's heartbreaking lament:

'Fear no more the heat o' the sun,
Nor the furious winter's rages;
Thou thy worldly task hast done,
Home art gone, and ta'en thy wages:
Golden lads and girls all must,
As chimney-sweepers, come to dust.'

It is my turn. After three pages of Jonathan my eyes are watering. How on earth am I going to do this at the funeral in front of heaps of people? Dad comes up and says "Excellent – well done."

Maybe it will be all right. As long as I don't cry.

"Yes, well, something for everyone, a laugh, a cry, an anecdote."

Mum is still choked. Standing by the coffin she says: "Very good, remember to slow down" and once again I feel that loss inside the pit of my stomach. This is the last time the five of us will be together in the same room.

Wir trauern nicht daß er gestorben ist, sondern
feiern daß er unter uns gelebt hat

Back home people in black start to arrive. Julie, Mum's sister, comes in and sits down in the rocking chair as if she has been there forever. Two colleagues from Jon's school drop off his two laptops and a video of him playing touch-rugby. They soon leave and Janet comes in to pray with us before we set out for the church. We all stand uncomfortably in the kitchen. It seems awfully formal.

We walk to the church, the police leading the way, followed by myself and Dad, Tobias and Mum with Hannah and Matthew following closely. People see us, nod tactfully, knowing where we are going. The Church, is packed, a mass of black. We hadn't discussed attire as a family but somehow we are out of the norm. I wear a black suit with a bright green jumper. Tobias wears a black-blue suit, Dad a brown coat and Mum has a blue scarf around her neck, the spirit of youth transcending through the blackness.

We walk down the centre aisle as the organ plays *Jerusalem*, an old Jonathan favourite and we sit down in the front pew. Before us to the left is a stand where people can light candles in memory of relatives and friends. A few are lit, but poignantly underneath is a shelf where some-one has left a copy of the local newspaper with a large picture of Jon smiling up at us. Dad starts to cry but I just stare at Jonathan's face, look-ing intently into his eyes as Janet welcomes the mass of people behind me. Tobias gives his Shakespeare poem, not that I hear any of it. I remem-ber he did a similar reading at my wedding and I didn't listen to that either. I just focus on Jonathan's smiling face.

It's going to be OK, I think. Jon smiles back at me "I'm sure it is" he seems to say. It is my turn. I walk up to the pulpit and breathe in deeply, looking out onto the mass of black. Taking in faces for the first time, scanning people for recognition, but I recognise nobody. It is just a sea of grief waiting for something about Jon that they can connect to. I look down and see a note that Tobias left: 'Go for it Tots'. I smile and start:

I think of Jon, my brother my friend.

I think of him as a mischievous child locking all the nuns in the Refectory and running off – the problem being they had all vowed an Oath of Silence.

I think of him getting drunk for the first time and being sick in the bath.

But these are distant childhood memories.

No longer the boisterous boy running about the village with Bob and Robin, or the spotty teenager at the Vienna International School, Jon matured into a comparatively quiet adult but it was clear to all that at Oxford Poly – sorry Jon, Oxford Brookes University – he was having a whale of a time, the Drama Society, the OTC, the Edinburgh Fringe, organising balls. At the same time forging friendships for life with Jem, Richard and Chris. They all dabbled with humour and produced their own video sketches.

The Pendley Shakespeare Festival was Jon's thing. Tobias and I participated for a few years but that was what Jon did from the age of eight every summer. After a brief stint of acting he soon ingratiated himself as indispensable in the production team. Year in and year out he would help with the lighting and eventually he ran the lighting. Anything that involved possession of a walkie-talkie and he was your man. He knew he had made it when they let him stay for free at the Pendley Hotel.

After University Jon tried working in industry but soon realised that his forte was facilitating others. So he became a History teacher at The Duke of Kent School in Surrey. The heaps of former pupil letters pouring in hold testament to how fond they were of him and an example to us all of how a good teacher can make a difference to people's lives.

By then I had completed my teaching certificate and the nice thing was that, having been to the same university, he followed suit and did a similar PGCE. We lived together in Aldbury for two years, as he stayed on to teach at Ashlyns School.

It was during that time that Jon gave me an example of unconditional love. I was very angry at him once and shouted: "You're lying to me". He looked at me in complete disbelief. "Why would I lie to you?" And I realised then that there was no pretence, no prejudice between us, just acceptance of who the other person is.

I remember those days well, for if he wasn't working at the pub he was either playing dominoes or bridge. Every night at the stroke of nine he would go past saying "I'm off to the pub!" He loved working behind the bar and would even do a stint on New Year's Eve when he was back from teaching abroad – he did like a pint of Pride, or two.

You must understand that Jon wasn't a loud person, he had a dry sense of humour. He would say something and just leave it out there for you to catch. Then a large Cheshire cat smile would appear on his face; a grin that would also charm many a woman.

Jon had friends, not acquaintances. Everywhere he went he would forge a life-time friendship which he would honour and re-visit, regardless where he went. Others would consider him with respect, maybe, a bit of a grump, but they were looking from afar and didn't know him. Those who knew him knew they were the lucky ones.

I think of Jon at the Bavarian International School and then at the Ho Chi Minh International School, organising and co-ordinating not just within his job but forever being part of whatever production was taking place. Quite a few of his colleagues will remember him not only for his wit but also the one side of his shirt hanging out at the end of the day. He was dedicated to his work, in school most Saturdays. This didn't stop him from having fun once the work had stopped, his most recent sport being touch-rugby. He had also been made Director of Studies at Ho Chi Minh, and had grand plans of what to do next. We had a secret plan of our own: one day we would work in the same school where he would be Head.

In Munich Jon started to develop a new talent. Like his father he had a lovely baritone voice and he became a bit of a crooner. When meeting up with Chris in the holidays they would attach themselves to the piano and sing. He had recently been invited to sing a solo at a ball, he was considering a Bond number. Munich was also where he became firm friends with the Australian couple Shane and Mel.

Jon's home was Aldbury, it was his recuperating place. He would go out into the world, work and play hard and then come back to Aldbury to flop. Here was his family; he would bounce in and drag my husband off to the pub, he would sit in the garden with his arms behind his head and feet up on a chair. Aldbury was his family, his friends and his home and in the summer it was Pendley. I don't think there is anyone who can imagine the Pendley Shakespeare Festival without Jon. This summer he reached what was in his eyes the pinnacle of success: the role of Assistant Festival Director, a walkie-talkie in his hand while wearing a DJ.

I think of Jon arriving at Bali, full of beans, just as he would be when arriving here for Christmas. Full of bounce, ready to catch up and have fun with Shane and Mel prior to the IB conference. There was nothing he liked better than a jolly.

I think of Jon dumping his bag and waiting for Shane, sitting on the veranda of the hotel with his arms up behind his head and his big belly protruding. I think of them walking to the Sari Club, putting the world to rights, for Jon was a serious person who had serious opinions. I think of Jon drinking his beer and it all suddenly being over.

Shane and Jon were very close. I take comfort from the fact that this year Jon had been the happiest he had ever been, and he died doing what he liked doing best (apart from walking around with a Walkie-talkie in his hand) having a beer with a friend.

It is a lovely service. Janet reads out letters from past pupils, friends and colleagues. Richard gives a reading from the first Letter to the Corinthians, Chapter 13:

...meanwhile these three remain, faith, hope and love and the greatest of these is love.

Our friend Hugh sings *A wandering minstrel I* from *The Mikado*. Jon's first ever public singing solo at the age of ten: although he continued to sing it in his bath.

Mum in Austria attended a funeral where those attending all had a flower to throw into the grave. So there are flowers for the congregation to collect in the porch. Everybody follows us, in a long procession, to the vast hole. There we touch the coffin one last time and it is lowered slowly to be covered by a mass flowers as, one by one, people from all walks of Jon's life stop to pay their own tribute and say goodbye.

We stand to the side as, one by one, people hug us. Old people, young people, friends, colleagues, relatives, past pupils, Pendley Shakespeare veterans, old friends even Jon hadn't seen for donkey's years.

Indeed it was a good funeral. Jon would have been proud, stunned in fact, by the amount of interest and the sorrow his death has caused. He would have liked the wake (what a contradictory word) as well, for it takes place at his other spiritual home, as Janet has put it in her address, at The Valiant Trooper pub.

At the end I stand there alone. Everyone has drifted off to the pub. Two men arrive and start to replace the soil. It is so pretty swamped with flowers. "Do you have to do that now." I ask.

"I'm sorry, we've been told to, they don't want no press coming over here." I can't hold on to my coffin forever and, after all, isn't Jon's spirit still in Bali?

I walk down Trooper Road alone, fully aware that Jon and I have taken this path so many times together. Taking a deep breath I walk in. The place is heaving, with that familiar smell of beer, and loud noise. All around the pub are pictures of Jon at different stages of his life. Well done, people keep saying to me, as if I've just come off stage. "I don't know how you did it". "Well, you just do it don't you" I say. The Ellwoods have always been putting on the show. All of us involved with some form of entertainment, whether a production, a party, a play or even a wedding. It is in our blood and I guess Jon's funeral lives up to what we are. Somehow that is all this seems – a show. It is there for the others, a public service so that they can have a chance to feel the pain, openly share the emotions that go with death and, I suppose, ultimately let go and move on.

Of course, many are here to show their support, not just to Jon but also to our family, To show how important he is to them and indeed it is wonderful to see so many people. But momentarily it seems so flippant, all these people packed into the pub, catching up on old times, sharing Jon stories and then saying goodbye, stepping into their cars and back into their lives.

But once they are gone we are left alone with our grief, to cope, to cry and come to terms with this atrocity that has ripped Jon away from our lives. Does unconditional love mean you also allow them to die? What about this heaviness that sits inside you, that makes you constantly feel that you can't breathe. Will it ever lift?

"Apparently it can take two years to get over a death of a close relative" someone says to me.

"So what happens after that?" I ask

"I guess the numbness lifts. Time is a great healer."

Hours later, I am one of the last to leave the pub. I gather up pictures of Jon and carry them home. Matt has long gone, with jetlag catching up on him. My emotions are raw. At home my anger rises up. It has been a good funeral, yes, something for everyone, not a dry eye in the house, but it doesn't bring my brother back. Mum seems alright. She says that Jon is with her now. "My little boy has come home" she says.

No I argue vehemently, Jon isn't here, all this means nothing, the funeral and the praying. He's dead, I felt him, in a cold, black bag, dead, just something heavy in a bag. I want to cry but somehow I can't. I am just angry now, I feel so helpless. We are standing in the kitchen, surrounded by flowers, letters, the night, totally and utterly shattered.

"Yes, but his spirit isn't in that bag is it?"

"No, it has been erased, like an ant being squished, that's it, no more Jonathan."

Mum isn't a great believer in the afterlife but she does believe that a person's spirit lives on, just like the love, from all over the world, that had wrapped around her, keeping her going after the bomb.

"Well, I'm sorry Mum, but as far as I'm concerned there is no God, no Heaven, nothing. It's just over and that is it." And so my previous belief system falls apart for I had felt death in my own arms.

For many, belief in the after-life helps them sort it all out, it makes sense. If you believe in Heaven or re-incarnation then you make it easier for yourself. Having a funeral is also a good thing: you need a function at which you can openly celebrate someone's life, openly cry at their departing and voice your sorrow. However just like everyone else who has lost someone close to them, I realise it is just a stepping stone on the journey of grief. Janet told me a story by Mary Stephenson about someone on a beach and feeling as if God has left him:

****

"You promised me Lord, that if I followed you, you would walk with me always. But I have noticed that during the most trying periods of my life there has only been one set of footprints in the sand. Why, when I needed you most, have you not been there for me?"

The Lord replied, "The years when you have only seen one set of footprints, my child, is when I carried you."

****

Well, if he's carrying me he's being very quiet about it.

28th October

I don't visit the grave again for a long, long time. Every time I drive past the church it is there in the corner of my eye. Mother visits nearly every day and has planted flowers on it. Others visit to ask for peace, leave more flowers with a message or a gesture of affection. On Christmas Day, Tobias even puts a Christmas cracker on it. On birthdays, family or festive days Mother lights a candle, a shining light of hope in the dark.

Matt and I are flying home to Penang, where our children are waiting with so small an understanding of where their parents have vanished to. On the way to the airport we have an important meeting to attend. Jack Straw would like to meet us and apologise in person. I voice my Mountain to Mohammed line again, but I am ridiculed. Our Foreign Secretary can't just arrive in our garden by helicopter.

Tobias is keen to meet and discuss the experiences we have gone through, and do something positive. He wants to put forward the idea of an Emergency Response Team for similar crises and also discuss the British Government's assessment of terrorist threats to that area. If the threat assessment had been raised to high then Jonathan, who was attending an official IB conference, would never have been in Bali as the meeting would have been cancelled.

Kevin and Jerome drive us up to London, baggage and all, for Matt and I are flying off that afternoon. We arrived at the Foreign Office at midday and park outside the entrance on an empty road. No-one comes and asks why we are parked right outside the Foreign Office. We sit there for 15 minutes, waiting to go in. So much for security.

Once through the door however, Tobias and I go through a huge palaver of security, as we have our photos taken, visitor's badges made and body checked. The Foreign Office is a grand palace, with a large quad in the centre where everyone parks. We follow our guide along long, high corridors of marble with grand staircases, centuries of history packed into the building. As you walk, you feel you are in an important place. On each side are large oak doors. Nobody seems to be around, all busy no doubt, putting the world to rights according to the British point of view. We continue up an imposing staircase to a carpeted, regal ante-room. Through the window we could see another giant quad leading to No 10 but only very special people can use the back gate.

We are offered coffee and stand around waiting – there is giant velvet sofa you could get lost in if you sat down. There are newspapers on a table, grand pictures of famous politicians looking down. Tobias is more used to this atmosphere, for it is really just like being at Sandhurst or in a posh Officer's Mess. To me it feels like visiting a stately home, waiting for the guide to show us the next room.

In the next room is Jack Straw, or so I assume. When he comes through to greet me I see he is a short man with grey hair, glasses and a broad smile. He walks straight up to us and shakes our hands firmly. Tobias towers over him.

Tobias has briefed me beforehand. "I'm going to talk about putting together a proper team and improving the structure of help available. You talk about how grateful we are for what help we did get."

"OK. Do you think he will know that you are from the other side?"

"Of course he will, he will have been briefed about us"

"Well, he won't have been briefed on me. I'm a nobody."

"I'm sure he'll soon work out you're a tree-hugger. Anyway it's very important that this isn't political. This is about Jonathan and what could have been different."

As it is, we needn't have worried. Jack Straw is open and friendly. He clearly has a mission, to be fulfilled in a very short window, which is to apologise and have a cup of tea with us. I'm not sure he is quite prepared for Tobias's candid and detailed approach.

Jack Straw's sofas are made of red leather. It is a very nice office, very spacious, with large windows, a mammoth oak desk at one end and his coffee table in the middle. Tobias sits down in a leather chair, and I sit next to him on the non-sinking sofa. To my right is the Right Honourable himself. Tobias meets people like this all the time, but this is my first politician. Not only that: he represents what I voted for. This is cards on the table time; is he going to come up trumps and show that he was worth my trust?

To Jack's right is the officer in charge of the crisis at the Foreign Office end. To her right is Jack's secretary, a neat, young man who nods at Jack every so often. "First of all let me say, how deeply sorry I am about the loss of you brother in these tragic circumstances…"

He offers more than we expect and gets straight to the point concerning the assessment risk. He explains about security information and the problem of interpreting medium and high risk. At present he is still looking into whether the Foreign Office could have done more and raised the warning. They still seem to be sitting on the fence on this issue.

Tobias discusses his ideas for improving the situation for the future. Soon it becomes an intelligent discussion about what training people need to cope with these events, not only within a specialist task force but also for honorary Consulate staff, who may have no idea what to do in a crisis. There is no hand-book, no guidelines, and they shouldn't have to learn it on the hoof. Tobias starts to quote the statistics about the defence budget and once again I think Jack Straw is surprised at how assertive we both are. I tackle him about the Ambassador's absence. Once again Jack Straw is apologetic and agrees that the top man should have stayed and not returned to Jakarta.

He is a concerned man. Despite being in a hurry to get to *Question Time* in Parliament he overruns his time with us and seems genuinely interested in the problems we faced. We make a point of mentioning people like Mark Wilson and David Magson, who should be rewarded for their hard work after trying so hard to make things easier for us. (Both were eventually in the Queen's Birthday Honours list.)

We also insist that the British government still needs to help the British victims' families more. Only yesterday, we spoke to someone whose brother had died and he is getting minimum help to get out there or even cope with the situation. Mr Straw points out that this is quite a new situation for them. Tobias stresses again that lessons need to be learnt so other families aren't let down. Mr Straw invites him back to address a team about the lessons learnt from Bali.

At least that is a start.

30th October

Going to Vietnam

Once a funeral is over, a line is drawn and the family is left to get on with it. 'It' often means sorting out the deceased's effects. All of Jon's effects were in Vietnam and a member of the family was asked to attend a memorial service. I had moved to Malaysia because it was close to Jonathan. It had made my initial transition into the world of International teaching seem easier at the time. If something went wrong Jon was around the corner. I didn't realise fate had it the other way round.

So after a night with Felicity and Freddy in Penang, I am back at Kuala Lumpur airport waiting for my flight to Vietnam. I still have a sense of the world revolving around me while I seem static. Despite travelling my insides feel as if they haven't moved and why on earth do all these people not know that my brother is dead?

I am sitting on my seat waiting, flights coming in, flying out, the place is buzzing with people and I realise that the world has shifted. Everything looks different, everything has changed. I can't quite see how, it's still blurred. I think of the butterfly that flutters its wings on one side of the world and the chain reaction causes an hurricane on the other. I look down at the newspaper on my lap. The headline is 'Mount Etna Volcano'. Lava is pouring out into a Sicilian ski resort. The last line reads: 'People do the only thing they know how to do (and can do) – pray!

My sense of blur is still with me as I walk through Ho Chi Minh City airport. Glass corridors skirt the entire length of the airport until you arrive in a vast waiting hall where, without a visa, you will not be allowed to enter the country. They are sticklers for bureaucracy here, but after Bali nothing phases me.

Am I actually entering a communist state? Images of *Platoon* and *Good Morning Vietnam* skim my mind. I know little about this country. Jonathan was the historian and took a delight in living in the country he had taught about in such depth.

I can't get past the visa-officer without an official address and a telephone number. I have an address but no telephone number, so I just make one up and get through that way. He asks me why I am visiting and I start explaining once again. He doesn't bat an eyelid, doesn't even give me an 'I am sorry for your loss'.

Outside Derek Rutt, Jon's friend and colleague from the school, is waiting with their local business manager in case there are problems. Derek clearly knew Jon extremely well. They lived in the same complex and have spent many an hour chewing the cud in some Saigon bar or other. He ushers me into a people-carrier; echoes of arriving at Bali and leaving another airport shudder through me.

Ho Chi Minh is not unlike Penang, with hustle and bustle, too many cars and motorbikes on the road, heat, dirt and atmosphere that seems to come hand in hand with an Asian country, and I am in my third in the space of two weeks. Ho Chi Minh has more mopeds, and bicycles and tri-shaws than you can ever imagine, with cars few and far between.

I am staying at the Caravelle, central hotel opposite the Ho Chi Minh Opera House where Jon had stage-managed the school's production of *Tartuffe*. At least I am seeing some of the places Jon knew so well. We drop my bag off and Derek takes me to a bar. He is very considerate, obviously making an effort to show me some of Jon's life. Wherever we go he points things out: "Jon would have walked along these streets on many an occasion." Pointing out a bar he says "Jon would frequent that one", "we enjoyed going there". But he is finding it hard, he is still in shock.

We talk about the news. A club has burnt down in a building where an air-con had gone wrong and 100 people were dead. In Russia an extremist group has taken the audience in a theatre hostage. The Russians, in an attempt to deal with the situation, inadvertently gas nearly 150 people and kill them. Another 250 people removed from this, our world, but I am immune to it. Death still has me by the scruff of my neck and is stifling my emotions.

In the Caravelle Hotel I change for the memorial service. I put on my flowery dress and a pink t-shirt. I refuse to be the dark mourner and want people to know that I celebrate Jonathan and always will.

We take a taxi to the New World Hotel; more traffic, more mopeds, little progress on the road. In the foyer bar Derek shares some Dutch Courage with me and I meet Sean O'Maonaigh, the Headmaster, a large gentleman with a broad smile. He is under much stress, for another friend of his has died in the air-con fire that day. He shows genuine gratitude that I have made the effort to attend.

We walk up the stairs to the large conference hall where the event is taking place. At the top of the stairs is a sign saying 'A Celebration of Jon Ellwood', pointing onwards. I gulp, the blur is subsiding. This time I am on my own. Students are milling about and I start to regret my choice of pink, for everybody is in black. I can't change now, but it does make me stick out.

We are a little early. The hall has seats for about 200. To the left is a massive screen with a picture, two metres by three, of a vast, smiling Jonathan, with a twinkle in his eye which seems to say 'look at me.' I try to pull myself together.

I am not expecting this. My heart is pounding. This is worse than the funeral. That was almost abstract compared to this.

We walk to the front where there is a small stage with a backdrop which says, in gold, three-dimensional letters 'A Celebration of Jon Ellwood 30th Oct'. This is the school's farewell to Jon. It has been such a shock for them. One day their teacher is there, the next they are bereft. Teenagers study wars in history, they debate internationalism in class and now they are faced with a reality they don't really understand. It has broken their daily routine and this is their chance to let go and move on.

I already have a sense of the grief the school is going through. As at the Bavarian International School, Jon and Shane had both made an impact on the students that they would never forget. Both schools arranged memorial services and both schools sent countless letters of condolence, from students, staff and parents with story after story of what Jon had meant to them. In a macabre way it is like an advertisement of 'what is a good teacher?'

The service opens with footage of Jon at the IB weekend he had organised, showing him climb a cliff and abseil down. Sinatra's *My Way* accompanies it. The programme is punctuated with Jon's favourite songs, either songs he had sung or songs that summed him up. From *Memory* sung by the staff to the *Bare Necessities* sung by the students, followed by Sting's *How fragile we are*, it is the soundtrack of Jon's life, all effectively chosen. Talk about not a dry eye in the house. If the speeches don't make you cry the songs break your heart. I have three tissues and they are sodden and all this with Jon grinning down at me mischievously from the screen.

Andrew Derham, the Secondary School Head, gives a speech in which he says "Jon made this school a better place." He is followed by Zoe, a pupil. A touch-rugby mate of Jon's makes us all laugh with some Jon witticisms, but then brings us crumbling down again as he shows footage of Jon scoring a touch-rugby try. They play it again in slow motion and I really wonder if I am going to be able to stay in the room, let alone give a speech.

Sean O'Maonaigh reads a poem about time. Then once again, I am faced with the prospect of standing up in front of a crowd of people who want something, need something of Jon. I am saved by the sound of Jon's voice; his dulcet tones had been recorded at his teaching week-end singing *From Russia with love*. There is my Jon standing with his friend, Dave, on the guitar. He isn't looking up, he is too busy concentrating on the words, but he is grinning and loving it, as are the pupils in the film watching him. It is touching but he does sound quite out of tune. I can't help but laugh. The song finishes and Jon's broad smile descends on us again and once more I know I can do this. After all, it's simply talking about my brother.

I have adapted my funeral speech, although this time I feel I want to say a little more. This is an International school, we have grown up with this family and the 'international' part of the Ellwoods is integral to our everyday life.

...Nobody here will forget Jon Ellwood. We are all too involved. However the disbelief and pain will gradually ease. In months, years, maybe even ten years down the line, you will remember your teacher, friend, colleague Jon Ellwood with fondness and a sense of injustice. Remember then, that he is an example to us all of how we should live our lives. 'Seize the day', carpe diem, as he did, for no-one knows what the future may bring.

As one of his students said: 'He was not just a teacher, he was a teacher of life' – what greater complement could a teacher have?

This atrocity has left many in a state of disbelief. Our perspectives of the world have shifted, some to disillusionment. Think of Jon Ellwood's life not as a waste but as a promise for your future, to strive to live in peace and tolerance.

I finish with a quote from my mother's article in *The Independent*.

I leave you with the story of Pandora who opened the fateful box and released a seething mass of beastly horrors onto humankind. The age of innocence was gone but as the world wept, Imperial Zeus looked from the sky and gave his final gift… of Hope.

The worst part is over. Everyone walks out of the dark room, slowly into the light of the foyer. Students cry, staff look sad, waves of grief flow as they stand around, tentatively eating the refreshments provided. Pupils with tears rolling down their young faces come up to me, wanting to say something but then faltering in shyness as they realise they don't know what to say to this sister of Jon's, a complete stranger. Some seem scared to approach me and just watch from afar.

"I'm sorry" a woman says. "He was very happy here" I respond.

"Thank you for allowing me to come here and get a slice of his life" I say to another. "I'm honoured to be here" I offer. "No, no we are the ones who should be honoured." It becomes quite surreal.

Eventually we leave and go to a bar, conveniently on the roof of my hotel and aptly named Saigon Saigon. More faces, more sympathetic smiles, these are Jon's good friends now, people who knew him well, knew him happy, knew him sad. Bruce, Calvin, Timmy, Louise… all with a story about Jon and a look of disbelief that he was gone. Friends tell me things I never knew about Jon, others support stories I've heard him tell.

****

Dear Caroline, Peter, Totty and Tobias

It is so very difficult to write this letter and express all the emotions that come with such a tragedy. I'd simply like to let you know that I miss Jon very much.

I joined the International School at the same time as Jon and we became great friends as well as colleagues. I was always impressed with Jon's determination to do anything he did well and this is particularly memorable during his IB Information evenings. These were a huge success and many parents and students became more informed about the IB diploma as a result. The sound, lighting and Jon's own presentation and delivery were scrutinised, corrected and reworked until Jon was happy. This took time but the end result was a polished, thoughtful and highly informative evening. These were jokingly dubbed 'Ellwood Productions' and gained Jon great respect.

I travelled with Jon to Cambodia for a holiday in April 2002 to explore the wondrous temples of Angor. This was a great trip and many laughs we had along the way. It seems very odd to say that I feel lucky now to have made the trip with him. He was a great travelling companion and certainly got us organised whilst remembering that we were on a holiday after all. A really lovely few days away from the hustle and bustle of Saigon that will live long in my memory.

It is a terrible shame that the lives of many students and teachers will never be enhanced by the talents of a man whose ability and drive to do great things in International schools around the world. His ambition was to lead a school and I believe he would have made a superb job of it.

Jon was a great friend and there will always be a very fond place in my heart.

Yours sincerely, Calvin Curtis

****

Suddenly I've had enough. I don't want to be here anymore. These are nice people but I can't take it. I can't share him anymore. It is getting too much. I can't bring him back, no matter how hard I wish for it. So I go to bed, for the next day will be my day, I will be going to Jon's flat.

31st October

Ho Chi Minh City School is relatively new, built only nine years ago in the suburbs of Saigon. I depart from District One and once again, escorted by a mass of mopeds all weaving their way to somewhere, find myself outside a very secure school behind a high wall.

Inside it is buzzing with activity, as all schools are. It is Halloween and the school is celebrating by dressing up. All the staff I had met the previous evening, then in black and with sorrowful faces, now walk around dressed up as witches, lions, clowns. Many see me and came up to say hello. It was quite hard to recognize some of them. We soon leave the hubbub and walk next door to the Riverside Apartments where about 40 percent of the staff live, as did Jon.

Derek explains that once Jon's demise had been announced the authorities had sealed his flat up and allowed no-one in. We go to the manager's office for the key, where we are met by a Vietnamese policeman over-seeing the operation. The shipping people are also due to pack everything up but I want some time in Jon's apartment before they arrive.

We walk back to Jon's block, where on the ground floor I see the effective sealing of his apartment door: they have locked it and placed soggy pieces of tissue along the seal of the door and door frame. I laugh, at least it is a gesture of security. The policeman ceremoniously removes the tissue and opens the door.

It is like entering a tomb. You know that everything in the room has lost its place, its purpose. Opposite the door is Jon's large, blue sofa which he had ordered last summer, a perfect fit for his width and length so he could loll on it and watch his surround sound TV in complete comfort.

To the right is his desk and shelving unit, his home office, with papers neatly placed to the side, shelves full of DVDs, files and books. Little piles of money await his return. I walk along the small corridor, past his tiny kitchen, still with washing-up sitting in the sink, to his bedroom, where his shirt hangs and his casual chinos lie neatly.

Derek turns to the police-officer who is hovering by the door, "Can you just give her a few minutes?" He agrees. Derek also takes his leave, allowing me to soak in some Jon. This is a part of my brother I don't know. Of course I recognise all the things, the type of toothpaste, the picture of Felicity on the wall, the clothes, the set-up of the massive TV as the main feature of his abode, even the smell, but it is emptiness that washes over me. These are just things, they mean little or they could mean everything, material everyday things that Jon used without a notion that one day someone else would be picking them up as the only connection they retain. Like his 'phone, I use it every day now, knowing that it was Jon's, but one day it will break, it will need upgrading and I will just have to let go all over again. So this is it, Jon, I think, it's time to close your chapter here.

It makes sense, no point dwelling on it. I open the cupboard and start to sort systematically through the clothes; clothes to keep, clothes to give-away, t-shirts that mean something, trousers that don't. The piles grow higher. Derek returns and starts to unwire the TV and the countless wires that Jon had carefully connected to create his home cinema.

The shipping people arrive and I sit and watch as parts of Jon's life are put into boxes. They clearly know the circumstances, for the Tiger removal people are very quiet and tactful.

In the kitchen I open the fridge, full of beer and soft drinks. Derek and I empty all the food into a box, along with junk it seems pointless to send home, easier to give away. He had six pots of Marmite in his cupboard to cover him for a year's stay in Saigon.

Next to a sink full of grubby dishes is an ash-tray, full of cigarette butts. I double-take: no, it can't be, my Jonathan doesn't smoke! Had he taken up smoking and not said anything? He wasn't smoking in the summer. I wrestle with the idea, it confounds me. Here is something I didn't know about him. I grow angry, how could he, after giving up so successfully, how dare he?

I get quite upset. Maybe I didn't know Jonathan as well as I thought I did. If he's taken up smoking and not told me what else has he done? It wounds me deeply, and it isn't as if I can have a go at him about it, because he's dead and won't hear me. Bloody hell, what was he playing at?

After washing up, Derek and I sit and watch the shipping people wrap memories of Jon up into packages. Jon's pens, pencils, candle-sticks, towels, all being whisked away to Britain, where my Mother and Tobias will have the task of opening up Jon's life again and spreading it about the house.

Then it strikes me. Bill Roberts had been staying with Jon the few days before he left for Bali. That's it, he must be the smoker. Indeed, Bill had been visiting Jon's school and had stayed on in Jon's flat while he went off to Bali. I sigh with relief and feel normal again. Your image of someone can be so easily tainted and when someone dies you don't want anything to warp it.

Eventually the flat is empty. We step outside through the heaps of boxes, sign the police report and go back to the school. I walk around a bit, look at classrooms where Jon taught, offices where Jon held meetings, talk to people who had grown used to having Jon as part of their daily routine, but they will soon adapt. People come and go in the international world and another teacher will replace him. I say goodbye to Andrew Derham. It is personal again; he is clearly going to cry, here is someone who feels it, who is truly missing him.

Standing in the staff room, looking at Jon's empty pigeon-hole, Derek interrupts my thoughts. He has news of Shane. They have identified his body and he is on his way back to Aussie. Another chapter is closing. Both Mel and Shane's Mother will be moving on at last.

Just before I leave Derek at the airport, he presses an envelope in my hand from a staff member. I wait until I get to the departure lounge before I open it. Listening to Jon's mini-disc player and his choice Sinatra songs with tears rolling down my cheeks I read the letter and it makes me so proud.

****

Dear Totty,

You were so brave last night. You made us think. You and your family will be in our thoughts in the coming days and years. My parents both dropped dead 12 years ago today. I thought I had been kicked by a horse. I cannot imagine your pain as your brother was murdered in his prime. He did so much in his short life. We will try to follow his example and your family's philosophy.

Kindest thoughts

Elspeth & Jim Campbell

****

Moving On

The next leg is not only home to my own family but also the beginning of my private journey through grief. Going back to work, surviving day by day, overwhelmed with thoughts of death; Jon in a body bag, hundreds of bodies swimming in and out of my dreams. Everyone copes with the aftermath of death in their own way; mine is to simply carry on. What would Jon have done if it had been the other way round? Probably the same, continuing to teach international understanding, continuing to breathe in and out day by day, hoping the numbness will eventually lift.

Every time I hear the word bomb my mind jumps to the Sari Club. Unfortunately it is so often used in every day language. Kids say "he's going to kill me if I don't do that"; someone else comments on enlarging a photo: "let's blow it up". Another comment grates my soul: "It's such a dump this place, the best thing you could do is drop a bomb on it". They don't know, they don't think, they don't realise that every moment of the day you are thinking about it and anything can trigger off the grief.

Gradually time does pass and other memories replace the cruel ones. You say his name and it doesn't hurt so much, you remember the good times, little moments make you chuckle and death's grip loosens. Other times when you least expect it, he catches you unaware and pulls you back into the abyss of pain.

Felicity asks me "Is Jonathan dead?"

"Yes" I answer sadly.

"Where is he?"

My heart sinks, I don't want to be a hypocrite and my belief system has been shattered. "I don't know" I respond, but this is not enough for a four-year-old.

"Is Jonathan in Aldbury?"

I can't avoid the topic. She obviously needs an answer, but I don't have it yet.

Is he in Bali? Is he in Aldbury? All I know is that even though I know he is dead, and have felt his death in my arms, he somehow seems to exist still. It's as if he went away on holiday and just hasn't returned, only this time we know he's not coming back. But it's more than that. It's in our hearts, it's in our conversation when we talk of him, Jonathan does live on for those who knew him. We don't have him anymore but we have his spirit and what he stood for, just as all the other Bali victim's families have the spirit of their loved ones, in the knowledge that they meant something to them and were lucky to have had them as part of their lives.

Finally I respond to her question. "He's up there in the stars, looking down on us." I hope that one day I will be able to give her a fuller answer.

Summer 2003

Somewhere, someone is planting bulbs on a grave. Somewhere, someone is scattering her husband's ashes into the deep blue sea. A mother is looking sadly at the happy picture of her child. A father is missing his son. A man stands inside a rugby club mournfully looking at pictures of strong men, lined up ready for their next tournament. Somewhere, someone visits a friend, learning how to live with amputation.

Somewhere in the world, on a small paradise island a family, a hotel, a school, a taxi-driver try to survive as their town struggles to recover from the aftermath of a bomb, a bomb that altered so many people's lives, that made people sit up and think about what they were doing, that pointlessly killed so many and wounded more.

A bomb that paradoxically reminds us that a peaceful world should be paramount to all, that international understanding is about recognising that differences exist. An eye for an eye doesn't work. Bombs, wars, and tragedy don't bring justice. The intolerance just carries on and certainly doesn't bring loved ones lost back.

Somewhere, someone else is making another bomb.

But some people know that no matter how many bombs they plan, no matter how many people they kill:

'No bomb that ever burst
Shatters the crystal spirit'

(George Orwell, see
p4 for further details)

96

Appendix One
'Fear no more the Heat of the Sun'

As relatives in Bali searched for the lost members of their families, those left at home waited anxiously for news. As through the intersecting webs of communication more and more people became aware of a particular loss, friends visited, letters of condolence and support arrived. It was this outpouring of love and affection that kept away total despair as the message came once again: "no hope yet of getting the body out" These golden lads and girls were not coming home.

Two international school teachers were known to be dead in the Bali bomb blast, two more were still missing and assumed dead and it was possible that more might be involved. Only slowly did the real picture emerge as many schools in the region were on half term holiday and the scheduled International Baccalaureate Regional Conference was cancelled, thus registration could not be checked.

International teachers are part of a global family and as the e-mails flew it became clear that it was a deeply wounded family. Teachers, parents, students all shared the grief and as memorial assemblies were planned questions were also asked. The first was a practical and political concern. If the International Baccalaureate Organisation had known that Bali was on the list of possible sites for terrorist activities in the area, surely the Conference would have been cancelled? So there was considerable anger as it emerged that the British and Australian Governments had known, but had failed to pass on the information.

The second question is a philosophical one. How can we continue to teach our students tolerance and multi-cultural understanding when the very teachers who pass on that message are blown up by terrorists? "Clearly", as one teacher from Vienna International School put it "our work to wipe out sectarian bigotry and violence is not yet done".

Indeed the Bali bombing becomes not just a clear symbol of the enormity of the task but also for many people a reason to say that task has failed and furthermore to identify the enemy as Islamic Fundamentalism. It is then but a short step, particularly for those who have no knowledge of the Islamic faith, to label all Muslims as terrorists.

If we are to maintain a philosophy of shared humanity, difficult though it may be in the present climate of terrorism; if we are to celebrate diversity and have a belief in the power of service (part of the Mission Statements of every international school), then we must be willing to study the history and culture of Islam in order to make considered judgements and not knee-jerk reactions to events. And if we are asking Islam to reconsider its fundamentalism, then the West must reconsider how genuinely liberal is its liberalism.

It is interesting in this context to consider the meaning of the word 'jihad'. Linked to a number of fundamentalist sects, some with a record of violence, the word has become almost synonymous with terrorism, yet its meaning is neither crusade or war but 'struggle'. As Karen Armstrong points out in her book *Muhammad, A Western Attempt to Understand Islam*, jihad is much more than fighting a battle, or a political struggle. It is also a personal, moral and spiritual commitment to conquer the forces of evil in oneself. An understanding of this word can thus illuminate how by extension it has brought some groups to believe that they have a mission to struggle, with whatever force necessary, against the forces of evil they perceive in many aspects of the West.

Understanding is the start, for from it can come an ability to confirm our own rights and beliefs whilst respecting the rights and beliefs of others. As Chinue Achebe says, we must allow the opportunity for others than Westerners to "celebrate our world, and sing the song of ourselves in the din of the insistent song of others".

Yet as we talked of tolerance, compassion and understanding the telephone still did not ring. How can we make the theory match the reality when Deborah Snodgrass, Jon Ellwood, Shane Walsh-Till and Jamie Wellington were all killed in Bali with maybe 200 others. Perhaps an answer can be found in the story of Pandora, who opened the fateful box and released a seething mass of beastly horrors onto humankind. The age of innocence was gone but as the whole world wept, imperial Zeus looked from the sky and gave his final gift... of hope.

Dr Caroline Ellwood, Oct 17th 2002.
Published in The Independent *on Oct 18th 2002.*

Appendix Two
Those Remembered

Australia

Gayle Airlie
Belinda Rae Allen
Renae Marie Anderson
Peter Carlo Basioli
Christina Betmalik
Matthew Lucas Bolwerk
Abbey Renae Borgia
Deborah Anne Borgia
Gerardine Buchan
Stephen James Buchan
Chloe Blanche Byron
Anthony Francis Cachia
Rebecca Marie Cartledge
Bronwyn Louise Cartwright
Jodie Patricia Cearns
Jane Roselyn Corteen
Jenny Norma Corteen
Paul William Cronin
Donna Loraine Croxford
Kristen Marianne Curnow
Francoise Rose Dahan
Sylvia Dalais
Joshua Kevin Deegan
Andrew Maurice Dobson
Michelle Gai Dunlop
Craig Jeffrey Dunn
Shane John Foley
Dean Richard Gallagher
Angela Sylvia Rose Golotta
Angela Simone Gray
Byron John Hancock
Simone Jane Hanley
James Barkeley Hardman
William Roy Hardy
Nicole Maree Harrison
Timothy Leigh Hawkins
Andrea Michelle Hore

Adam Lionel Howard
Joshua Ives Iliffe
Carol Jane Johnstone
David Richard Kent
Dimitra Kotronakis
Elizabeth Kotronakis
Aaron James Lee
Justin Graeme Lee
Stacey Maree Lee
Danny Robert Lewis
Scott Lysaght
Linda Eileen Makawana
Suzanne Ames Maloney
Robert James Marshall
David John Mavroudis
Lynette Patricia McKeon
Marissa Lee McKeon
Jennifer Ann Murphy
Amber Sue O'Donnell
Jessica Maree O'Donnell
Susan Lona Ogier
Jodie O'Shea
Corey James Paltridge
Bradley Charles Ridley
Benjamin Neil Roberts
Bronwyn Robyn Ross
David Cameron Ross
Kathy Ann Salvatori
Gregory Raymond Sanderson
Catherine Patricia Seelin
Lee Anthony Sexton
Thomas Singer
Julie Vida Stephennson
Anthony Scott Stewart
Jason Terrence Stokes
Behic Sumer
Nathan Gregory Swain
Tracey Ann Thomas

Clint Nathan Thompson
Robert Rex Thwaites
Charles Richard Van Renen
Jonathon Andrew Wade
Vanessa Anne Walder
Jodi Leigh Wallace
Shane Patrick Walsh-Till
Robyn Gai Webster
Marlene Doris Whiteley
Charmaine Margaret Whitton
Gerard Micheal Yeo
Louiza Zervos

Brazil
Marco Antonio Farias
Alexandre Moraes Watake

Canada
Richard Henry Gleason
Mervin Peter Popadynec

Denmark
Laerke Caecilie Bodker
Annette Ovrgaard Jensen
Lise Tanghus Knudsen

Ecuador
Marcillo Ana Cecili Aviles

France
Guillaume Breant
Lionel Henri Erisey
Manuel Mordelet
Anthony Jean Underwood

Germany
Bettina Christina Brandes
Udo Paul Hauke
Angelika Helene Kohnke
Alexandra Koppke
Claudia Dietlinde Theile
Marie-Cecile Wendt

Greece
Dimitris Panagoulas

Indonesia
Rudy Armansyah
Rahmat Arsoyo
Gusti Artini
Gede Badrawan
Komang Candra
Ketut Cindra
Tata Duka
Sulaiman Endang
Faturrahman
Hanny
Iqbal
Juniardi
Mochamad Khotib
Ni Kade Alit Margarini
Made Mertana
Mugianto
Aris Munandar
Kadek Ngartina
Mawa Nyoman
Kadek Beni Prima
Lilis Puspita
Imawan Sarjono
Ati Savitri
Jonathan Simanjuntak
Salwindar Singh
Achmad Suharto
Elly Susanti Suharto
Agus Suheri
Made Sujana
Wayan Sukadana
Kadek Sukerna
Ketut Sumerawat
Wayan Tamba
Destria Bimo Adhi Wibowo
Widayati
Made Wija
Ketut Nana Wijaya
Made Wijaya

Italy
Roberto Antonio Sbironi

Japan
Kosuke Suzuki
Yuka Suzuki

The Netherlands
Norbert Edgar Freriks
Sander Harskamp
Mark Antonio Schippers
Marjanne Van Lijnen Noomen

New Zealand
Jared James Gane
Mark Morton Parker
James Peter Wellington

Poland
Danuta Beata Pawlak

Portugal
Diogo Miguel Dantas Ribeirinho

South Africa
Godfrey Fitz
Craig Russell Harty

South Korea
Eun Jung Moon
Eun Young Moon

Sweden
Johanna Helene Bergander
Ulrika Louise Gustafsson
Karin Maria Ulrika Johansson
Linda Kronquist
Lena Carina Rafling

Switzerland
Pascal Michael Dolf
Sereina Liesch
Gian Andrea Rupp

Taiwan
Kuo Hui-Min

United Kingdom
Timothy John Arnold
Neil John Bowler
Daniel Keith Braden
Christopher Bradford
Jonathan Mark Ellwood
Lucy Sandra Empson
Ian Findley
Emma Louise Fox
Laura Danielle France
Mark Barry Gajardo
Thomas Edward Hanby-Holmes
Paul Martin Hussey
Christopher John Kays
Annika Kerstin Linden
Nathaniel Thomas Miller
Natalie Jayne Perkins
Peter Clifford Record
John Christian Redman
Stephen James Speirs
Michael Standring
Edward De Warren Waller
Clive Walton
Douglas John Warner

United States
Karri Jane Casner
Megan Eileen Heffernan
Robert Alan McCormick II
George Hamilton Milligan
Deborah Lea Snodgrass
Steven Brooks Webster
Jacob Cardwell Young

Three bodies were unidentified.

List supplied by the FCO.